T0065756

how to be a Wicked Witch

Good Spells, Charms, Potions and Notions for Bad Days

Patricia Telesco

A FIRESIDE BOOK
Published by Simon & Schuster
New York London Toronto Sydney Singapore

FIRESIDE
Rockefeller Center
1230 Avenue of the Americas
New York, NY 10020

FIRESIDE and colophon are registered trademarks
of Simon & Schuster, Inc.

Designed by Christine Weathersbee

Manufactured in the United States of America

1 3 5 7 9 10 8 6 4 2

Library of Congress Cataloging-in-Publication Data
Telesco, Patricia.
How to be a wicked witch : good spells, charms, potions and notions
for bad days / Patricia Telesco.
p. cm.
1. Witchcraft. 2. Neopaganism. 3. Magic. I. Title

BF1571.T43 2001
133.4'3—dc 21   2001023912

ISBN 978-0-684-86004-6

For information regarding special discounts for bulk purchases,
please contact Simon & Schuster Special Sales at 1-800-456-6798 or
business@simonandschuster.com.

To all the wonderfully wicked witches in my life—Dorothy, Betsy, Rowan, Maggie, Talyn, AJ, Arawn, Scarlet, Green, Jennie, Wes, Robin, Dawn, Walker, Wade, Dyanne, Don, Daniella, Tuan, and Danielle. All these people inspired this book by teaching me how to use humor as good soul food. And in keeping with good humor, this book is also dedicated to Otter and Daniel (I know where your sock is) and to Corwyn and T'sa (don't touch that!). It is truly a blessing to be part of this crazy, wonderful extended family.

contents

Contents

⊰ Chapter Five ⊱
The Wicked Witch's Knapsack (Portable Magic)   137

The Advantages of Magical Tokens
Clarifying Terms
Applying the Art
  Numeric Correspondences

⊰ Chapter Six ⊱
Bubble, Bubble, Toil and Trouble (Food and Beverage Magic)   167

The Crafty Kitchen
Beverages
  Ingredient Correspondences
    for Wicked Potions
  Potion Components and
    Magical Correspondences
  Recipes
Foods
  Ingredient Correspondences
    for Wicked Foods
  Food Components and
    Magical Correspondences
  Recipes

Afterword   201

How to Be a Wicked Witch

⊰ introduction ⊱

Keep cool and you command everybody.
—St. Just

 M agic is in the air. All around the world right now people just like you are casting spells, making charms, concocting potions, fortune-telling and generally getting witchy! Why? Well, the reasons vary. Most seek some metaphysical help in meeting common human needs like finding a companion, opening the way for better jobs, increasing finances, spicing up their love lives, toning down tension and promoting a little extra luck when the mundane methods fail. For these individuals, witchcraft has become a personalized, meaningful way of bringing spiritual vision and power into everyday life and transforming it for the better, and it can be the same for you.

But what happens to the same well-meaning witches and weavers of spells when they get frustrated, depressed, irate, jealous or otherwise offended—what happens when life's apple cart gets overturned by an adversary or rival? Do they simply sit back, smile and take it nonchalantly on the cheek? Or do they decide to wield magic like a weapon, beating back the tide of proverbial manure that life often dishes out?

This question lies at the heart and soul of what every magical practitioner faces every day. There are two basic rules that most witches follow religiously: 1. Harm no one, including yourself; 2. Don't manipulate anyone's free will unless you want to experience the three-fold law firsthand (i.e., whatever you send out comes back three times). These rules don't leave us a lot of room for biting back or getting even because no one wants that negativity boomeranging!

So the question becomes: How can witches use spiritual, metaphysical aptitudes as a coping mechanism for life's bumps and bruises without overstepping the boundaries of sensible, positive magic? One good hint about this comes to us from a Chinese proverb that says "the fire you kindle for your enemy often burns yourself more than him." Wicked witchery recognizes this truth. The philosophy that How to Be a Wicked Witch advocates is one of preparedness . . . being ready for the fires when they come so you don't get burned, and knowing how to put them out afterward!

Preparedness is where this book begins—learning to talk the talk, walk the walk and know your art inside and out. We'll look at basic rules for wicked witchery, adding a healthy dose of humor to keep things in perspective. Even when life seems miserable, laughter is still a terrific medicine and a potent magic whose potential shouldn't be underestimated—but we're certainly not going to stop there!

How to Be a Wicked Witch then goes on to provide creative, clever, tactful and effective magical methods for handling many of life's hot situations, frustrations, disappointments and shortcomings. The next time you get downsized, dumped on by a friend or family member, jilted by a lover or just want to make the best of a bad situation, turn to *How to Be a Wicked Witch* and see what tidbits of advice you can find. Taking action in itself will improve your demeanor, and the activities suggested are neatly designed to keep your spiritual dignity intact.

When you're sad, depressed or downright irate, there really is a magical answer to your situation. The metaphysical techniques presented throughout this book use imaginative, meaningful components that allow you to take back the reigns of control in your life. In the process, if you follow my lead, you won't blow your karmic bank account either.

So when life's road is dotted with potholes, fill them with witchery! It won't solve all the problems we face, but it will make you feel better and help you smile again, which wins half the battle. Once you realize that you can make a difference in your life, you *can!* Start right now by pulling out your broomstick and flying to the nearest cozy chair where you can read more. Join me in making some proactive, life-affirming magic today!

one

Follow the Yellow Brick Road: Prep Work

It's now or never. You must live in the present,
launch yourself on every wave,
find eternity in the moment.
—Henry David Thoreau

Being a witch isn't something that necessarily comes to folks naturally. In fact, when most people think of a "typical" witch, they end up picturing scenes from *The Wizard of Oz*. Thankfully this stereotype has nothing to do with modern witchcraft. Witches in today's nine-to-five world aren't evil hags, nor are we necessarily as sweet as Glinda. In fact, we're actually fairly normal folks—people who have rediscovered our ruby slippers and the magic within, and then taken both into our personal Kansas in meaningful ways. No yellow brick road was necessary!

After reading this, your next natural question might be, "So what's up with the book's title?" If modern witches aren't really wicked, how can anyone become a wicked witch? The answer is that wicked witchery is not so much a stereotype as it is an emerging metaphysical philosophy.

See, wickedness (in this context) is not so much about being mean. It's about meaning what we BE. To explain, there are a lot of people in the world who still haven't realized they're sacred beings who deserve the best that life has to offer. While we give lip service to this ideal, few of us really put the principle into action. The art of wicked witchery activates this principle and goes one step farther. It puts it to the test regularly.

With that in mind, preparing for our role as a modern-minded witch starts with purging defeatist attitudes and replacing them with proactive spiritual vision. Since magic is to bend and change, we might as well begin with the negative patterns of our lives. From this point forward we will no longer fall victim to vicious circumstances, react hastily to another's jibes, be a wallflower or act like a wimp. No one ever said Pagans had to be pansies, and there is absolutely no reason why we shouldn't use magical energy to make the best out of seemingly impossible situations. The trick is doing so with cunning and wisdom.

Step One:
Bearing and Alertness

Before you can really sink your teeth into wicked witchery, you first have to learn how to curb the temptation to react and emote. Metaphysics requires self-control. There is a time and place for such things, but it's seldom when you're standing face to face with adversity. Rather than falling apart or having a temper tantrum, it's much wiser at this point to save your energy and use it for magickal manifestation! Besides giving you more power with which to work, this also gives you the tremendous satisfaction of knowing the "other guy" didn't get your goat! Additionally, an air of confident self-regulation says to any would-be gainsayers that "enough is enough." Without so much as a word, the vibrations in your aura communicate this to others who, in turn, will be far less likely to mess with you.

The Fearless Glamoury

Glamoury is the art of mystical illusion; not stage illusion like pulling rabbits out of hats, but auric illusion that shifts the energy in and around your body. This shift creates a specific atmosphere designed according to your need.

Witches use glamoury like spiritual armor. When various situations arise in which the individual feels unsuited to the task or circumstance at hand, he or she dons a glamoury filled with confidence, bravery, attractiveness, strength or whatever other energies suit the moment. This way, even when the inner well is lacking, the auric field around the witch expresses the right vibrations to handle things competently.

How do you do this, specifically to keep gossipers, hecklers and other unpleasant people from getting in your face? The best way is through visualization (which you can combine with the ideas for clothing magic discussed later in this chapter). You know the old saying "seeing is believing?" Well, that's what a visualization does for you. It builds belief, which in turn provides the power to make the glamoury work.

To start, try to visualize yourself as you are at this moment in detail. Now, think of a color or blend of colors that, to you, represents a fearless, but somewhat reserved attitude. Remember that you don't want to keep everyone away, just those whose presence disrupts your inner harmony. Many people find a combination of red (power) and white (protection) suits this visualization.

Once you choose your colors, envision them pouring down from above and wrapping your body in sparkling radiance. The light swirls clockwise around you, creating a shimmering shell above, below, left and right (think of a soap bubble made from lines of pure magical force and you'll get the idea). Keep the purpose of this energy strongly in mind all the while you're creating the imagery. You'll know you're doing this visualization correctly if you feel tingly or warmer than when you started. These sensations indicate a shift in personal energy, which is now being directed into an aura of magic.

The glamoury sphere moves with you everywhere because it is part of you and produced from you. If you wish, you can adapt this idea a bit and put a door or window in the visualized sphere so as to open the path for specific energies or people (or even to let yourself out) at intimate moments. I also suggest practicing this technique so you can bring up your glamoury and release it fairly quickly. Timing is everything, and there will be moments when you want that kind of presence snapped into place rapidly.

Waking Up and Staying Awake

Buddha once said that everything in life boils down to staying awake, and that's certainly true with our spiritual pursuits. One goal in developing witchery is to become alert, aware and fully present in our lives so we can out-maneuver the things that could derail us.

So, wake up! Be here, right now! Wicked witches recognize that if we're living in the past, in the "might have beens," we miss a lot. Even those of us living in the present waste an awful lot of valuable time wishing we were elsewhere—doing something or being with someone else—no matter how improbable that situation might be. Wishing has its place, but don't let it distract you from daily reality so much that life sneaks up and puts one over on you.

Start by paying very close attention to two things: your senses and the little voice within. Your senses provide ongoing information that's very important to moment-to-moment actions/reactions. An odd smell in the air, a sound, a touch, a flavor or a fleeting image can communicate worlds of insight without so much as one word ever being spoken. Now, however, instead of simply using your senses on a natural level, you're going to use them supernaturally.

You probably already do this without knowing it. For example, if you walk into a friend's house and immediately feel ill at ease, you might conclude that people there have been arguing. Here, because you were open to them, sensual cues jumped to a higher level and provided unexpected, and very helpful, insights.

Witches make this sensual jump to help with divinatory efforts, to choose spell components or magical tools, to find a coven with which to work and generally to keep us on our spiritual toes. To learn to do it yourself on a regular basis, here's what I recommend:

1. For an entire week focus on one of your five senses. Think about how the information you receive from that sense affects the way you feel, think, act and react.
2. Repeat step one with your four other senses. As you do, also consider how one sense seems to affect the others.
3. After this five-week period do a self-check. Do you feel more alert and focused? I'm willing to bet the answer is yes.
4. Now go one step farther by adding a meditation to the procedure. Sit comfortably and take three

deep, cleansing breaths. Pay attention to each of your senses one at a time. Extend them out in all directions, reaching ever farther. For example, you can feel the chair or ground underneath where you're sitting or standing, but what else can you feel? Can you feel the hum of a refrigerator, the vibration of a passing car, the subtle brush of a butterfly moving nearby?

As you do this, remember that there is no limit to how far your senses can reach in the astral plane. The astral landscape is the unseen world where magick resides. It is an in-between place where the distance between you and a star is but a thought.

5. Focus your sense on one specific thing. For example, if you're focused on the sense of hearing, listen to your breath or the wind. Note how the mood of this sound changes depending on the day, time or circumstances. These small changes are signals, so pay close attention.

6. Also pay attention to sounds, sights, feelings, et cetera that can't be easily expressed by words. For example, say you're extending your tactile senses toward another person's aura. As you encounter that energy, a sensation comes through—like smoothness, stickiness, static or whatever. This sensation represents the astral presence of the individual, and it won't lie to you (even if a glamoury is present). If you sense something wrong here, keep your distance!

7. Interpret these psychic impressions according to their symbolic value. For example, in point six a sticky aura might indicate a clingy personality or dishonest intentions, depending on what type of stickiness you're picking up. Only you can determine what these signs mean to you, but your psychic self will always use symbols to which you relate deeply. This is where listening to your inner voice becomes incredibly important.

You probably won't become an expert in extending your sensual awareness in one day, let alone a year. The idea here is to start a learning process and build on it at a pace that's comfortable and beneficial to you. Witches know that spiritual growth is highly personal and not to be measured by anyone else's ruler. The only measure that matters here is the one nestled in your soul.

What Ticks You Off?

If there's a downside to being awake and aware, it's that you become alert to everything, even those things that you might normally ignore. Thankfully, modern witchcraft advocates balance: for every down there's an up. In this case the upside is consistently recognizing those people and situations that tend to make you angry, insecure or otherwise out of balance.

Such individuals or circumstances can unravel the magic in your wicked witchery by pulling and pushing the right strings and buttons. But, because you've become more conscious of these people and situations, you can head them off or transform them with a little proactive magic! Here are two sample spells to try yourself or adapt to better suit your circumstances (for information on effective spell casting, see Chapter 4):

Keeping It Cool Spell

When you know you're going to be heading into a situation that's a potential hazard to your emotional stability, this amulet comes in very handy. All you need is an amethyst crystal small enough to carry with you. Amethyst is known for its ability to augment our powers of self-control.

Take the amethyst and put it in your freezer for three days during a waning moon (the waning moon emphasizes banishing). When you put it in the freezer, and each time you open the freezer door over the next three days, repeat an incantation like this one:

Never shall I play the fool;
Keep my wit and temper even and cool.

Carry the amulet with you into any loaded situations. In between uses, keep the crystal in your freezer to keep it charged with cool-headedness.

Back Off Spell

When I'm going into an environment where I want certain people to keep their distance, this spell has proven very effective. To try it yourself you'll need to prepare a personal aromatic oil of some kind (a scent that really speaks strongly of your personality), or a bottle of your favorite perfume or cologne. Empower this aromatic, saying:

Away from me all negativity,
_____ shall stay, away . . . away!

Fill in the blank with the name of the person who needs to back off.

Now, take this aromatic to where you see that person the most often. Dab it all around the area in which you stand or sit, quite literally marking your territory. Visualize strong white light pouring into each drop, thereby creating an invisible field of force that keeps out unwelcome visitors.

Confidence Chants: In typical New Age vernacular, these boil down to affirmations. An effective witch doesn't put himself or herself down, and always has a handy set of chants for all occasions as part of a working vocabulary. Immediately begin replacing phrases like "I can't" or "It's not possible" with something more positive and productive. For example, someone working on improving his or her self-image might use "I am important; I am sacred" as a confidence chant. One hoping to improve their love life might say "I am passionate; I am loving."

Once you've chosen a key phrase for the day, week or month, start repeating whenever and wherever possible. Say it when you're brushing your teeth, sing it while making coffee, shout it while driving to work. Each time you repeat these power words, they fill the air around you with magical vibrations that slowly seep into your aura and into your heart! Eventually you'll start listening to yourself and trusting the truth in your words.

By the way, if you don't feel comfortable with speaking out loud, or cannot due to circumstances, you can THINK the phrases instead. The thoughts of a witch are tinders for magic, and their energy shouldn't be underestimated. We are what we think, so think suitably witchy thoughts and become the magic!

Clothed in Magic

The witch is a multidimensional person who knows that people play many roles in life. So the question becomes: What kind of witch do you need to be today, and how do you "put on" that persona? One easy answer to this question comes to us through our wardrobe. After all, if clothes make the person, why not use the potent symbolism here for productive wicked witchery in a time-challenged environment? Wear that red suit for power, or pink when you need to be literally "in the pink"! If you're feeling particularly wicked, wear basic black (lots of it). Think Morticia Addams with even more attitude. It might sound silly, but people are turning to color therapists now to learn how the hues in and around our lives do, indeed, change the type of energy with which we have to work.

Remember that you can mix and mingle colors for slightly different effects, or use various shades to get the specific effect you want. To illustrate, bright yellow is more mentally active than pastel yellow. So if you're speaking to a large group, bright yellow is a good choice to project your ideas, and you might combine this with touches of red to project an air of authority. On the other hand, quiet, private conversations might be more suited to a pastel yellow theme with a hint of blue or pink to help the discourse flow smoothly.

Below you'll find a brief chart of color correspondences that you can consider in assembling your witchy wardrobe each day. As you ponder this, don't forget to blend in some other kinds of magic with your choices. For example, toss a bundle of blessed herbs into the dryer with your outfit to charge the clothes with sympathetic energy (this is especially effective for passion and warming up relationships). Or knot a spell into a shoelace and tie (bind the energy you need inside, then release the knot to release the magic). Really, the options are endless!

Color Correspondences for Wicked Witchery

Use this list as a reference tool when choosing suitable colors to augment a spell or ritual, in picking components for charms and amulets, in helping shift the overall energies in your home, in creating visualizations and in using other magical methods for which the associated symbolism might be helpful.

Black: A seriously wicked color that intimates similarly serious purposes and goals. Don't wear too much of this too often, as it can cause melancholy, but a periodic black suit, tie, shirt or robe can prove very useful in building the right attitude for wicked witchery. Also in some magical traditions, it's customary to wear black into sacred space during the fall and winter to honor the seasons and the changing amounts of sunlight.

Blue: Far more upbeat. This denotes a happy, contented witch who is not afraid to declare his or her joy and peace to anyone who cares to look. Darker blues are more restful in nature. Wear this shade when you need to maintain emotional balance or destress. Light blues build our sense of inner delight. Got a secret and want to flaunt it? Wear bright blue!

Brown: Very earthy and grounded. Brown communicates sensibility and firm foundations. If you're not about to be moved in life or in magic, wear brown in your wardrobe (especially shoes, which connect you to the earth).

Green: The figurative "go" signal. When you want to move ahead boldly (or give a would-be suitor an encouraging nudge to do so), this is the best color to choose. It's also an excellent choice when you're focused on personal growth or the development of a specific project.

Orange: Orange projects energy, but on a more friendly, mature level than yellow and red do by themselves. When you want to portray yourself as experienced, well-seasoned and well-rounded, this is a good color to add to your wardrobe. Keep the tones subtle; maturity rarely screams at people. It simply presents itself comfortably and confidently.

Pink: Pink is a healthy color, be it for mental, physical or spiritual wellness. It has power and loving energy like red, but on a far gentler level, making it a friendly hue. Pink is welcoming to old comrades and potential new allies alike. If you plan on working magick in a group setting, pastel pink is a good hue to help bring everyone into accord. Don't go too bright with pink, however. The screaming variety tends to make people notice the color instead of the person wearing it.

Purple: Purple is regal and learned. It has strong spiritual overtones that indicate you know your stuff and aren't the least bit afraid to put that adeptness into action if need be. Add this to your wardrobe and glamouries when you feel lousy or emotionally limp, but need to *appear* striking or distinctive.

The lavender shade of purple has strong watery undertones. This evokes peace, inner wellness and enhances your ability to go with the flow. An excellent choice when you feel the need to calm unwarranted fears, jealousy or an overly angry wicked witch.

Red: The color of passion, power, fiery zest and the energy of life itself. If your enthusiasm for wicked witchery starts lacking, or you feel as exciting as a wet noodle, red's the color you need. Warning: I don't recommend the workaholics out there add too much bright red to your daily finery. You'll end up volunteering even more than you do already, and overextend yourself! If you desperately need a little extra energy temporarily, go for a darker brown-red that provides some grounding and gently reminds you of your personal limitations.

Yellow: When you need to communicate your ideas effectively or give yourself a creative magical boost, yellow is a great helpmate. Yellow, especially a pastel shade, has strong affiliations with the element of air, which carries messages, wishes, encouragement and motivation. Brighter yellow is highly recommended for procrastinators, artists and witches who find themselves needing a refreshed perspective.

White: White seems to be the all-purpose color for magic. When you have nothing else that seems fitting, white's your fall-back color. Symbolically, white suggests an ambience of protection and purity. When you want people to know you're sincere, honest or trustworthy, wear white as a predominant color. Or add white to your wardrobe anytime you feel you might face a psychic, emotional, physical or magical attack. The vibrations in this color will help hold back some of the negativity. Also use it when you need to tone down your wicked nature in favor of quiescence.

Other ideas along these lines? Well, while today's wicked-minded witch wouldn't be caught dead in the fashions worn by our fictionalized predecessors, there was a special kind of power and presence evoked by the image of black hats, capes and robes. Why not take a cue from this and add some dramatic, assertive touches to your wardrobe, especially items that have personal significance. If someone you dislike at work commented unfavorably about a particular scarf, for example, wear it on purpose (keep your magical goal in mind when you put it on). This makes a silent statement to that person, one that will keep you smiling all day long!

And for heaven's sake, don't forget to accessorize! A witch without jewelry is basically naked (if you don't believe me, I dare you to go to any magical gathering and find more than one or two people not covered in rings, bangles and/or beads). Thankfully for witches with good fashion sense, New Age outlets, gift shops, magical merchants at gatherings and even science stores carry a wide variety of jewelry these days. You might have to do a little hunting to find a token that expresses your magical goals and doesn't screw up the budget, but it's worth the time. In the end you'll have an entire outfit that radiates your magic—from head to toe and out to the world.

Witchy Aromatherapy

In preparing for your role as a witch, there are a lot of things to consider. Among them are two facts: 1. You might not want everyone in the world to know about your choice of vocations; 2. There may be times when you don't want to advertise your private witchy ambitions, even among people with whom you might normally share ongoing magical projects. Thankfully, there's nothing that says witches have to hang out a billboard declaring their spiritual choices.

The beauty of aromatherapy is that it is marvelously subtle. Who thinks anything of a lingering perfume or cologne, a bowl of scented flowers, a desktop air freshener or a locker sachet? This certainly doesn't scream "witch" to passers-by! And, like a glamoury, the gentle scent of various aromatics transforms your auric atmosphere, so it bears the energy you most need when you need it and where you need it!

In working with aromatherapy, I recommend either making your own tinctures, potpourris, air fresheners and/or oils or buying natural products. Making your own aromatics instills the preparation with personal energy and willpower. My book *The Herbal Arts* has many recipes along these lines. For time-challenged witches, buying natural products is a sound alternative since it keeps chemicals that might hinder your witchery out of the equation. If you're not sure where to get natural fragrances, I recommend looking to herbal teas, natural food cooperatives, bath shops and New Age stores.

Here's a brief list of common aromatics and their correspondences for magic:

Aromatic Correspondence List

Basil: A tenacious aroma that encourages spiritual stick-to-it-iveness.

Bergamot: A confidence booster for wicked witchery or any uncertain circumstance.

Cedar: An antibug aroma to keep away insects even of the human variety.

Chamomile: A tranquil herb that brings everything back to an even keel.

Cinnamon: A power oil that also gets rid of really slimy individuals and cleans up fraudulent circumstances.

Eucalyptus: A healthy scent that provides extra protection when your body, mind or spirit is ailing.

Geranium: A flower filled with emotional balance; this keeps your body, mind and spirit in symmetry and harmony.

Grapefruit: A comfort herb for easing jet lag and energy drains from spell casting and ritual work.

Jasmine: A prophetic aroma that augments foresight. True to the wicked witch's outlook of forewarned is forearmed, wear this to keep your psychic powers activated.

Lavender: A peaceful scent that maintains tranquillity within and without. This also alleviates the blues.

Lemon: An excellent choice for banishing lethargy in yourself or others, or to augment cleansing and health.

Lotus: A blossom that emphasizes feminine attributes and improves intuitive ability.

Mint: An aroma commonly used to offset stress and the gnawing that occurs in your stomach around disagreeable people.

Patchouli: A balance to lotus, this emphasizes masculine attributes and improves contemplative abilities.

Rose: A friendly, loving aroma that spreads positive vibrations wherever you may be.

Rosemary: An herb of choice for memory retention (wicked witches NEVER forget) and ridding the air of negative vibrations.

Sage: A scent that ensures your magickal efforts will be long lasting. Also good to wear when you have difficult decisions to make.

Sandalwood: An oil that redirects our focus toward spirituality and magickal issues.

Vanilla: An aroma for the zesty wicked witch who wants some unbridled passion from within or without.

Verbena: A scent that improves overall comeliness and charm.

Vetiver: An excellent aromatic for shape shifting and glamoury work.

I should note that this list is generalized. The way you react to an aromatic may vary dramatically from this list, so trust your instincts. Also avoid any aromatic to which you may have an allergy. Sneezing in the middle of a spell does not make for great magic!

Life's Little Rule Book

Last but not least, you'll need to know some of the rules of wicked witchery. Wicked witches today, and in fact nearly all metaphysical practitioners, live by certain mottoes that are guidelines for the way we think and act so our magic manifests in more effective, fulfilling and life-affirming ways. These mottos have resulted from the magickal community's experiences (both good and bad), and our sharing of those experiences with our fellow witches.

Mind you, each person's version of this list might vary a bit (wicked witches are terribly independent sorts), but this generalized overview will serve to get you started.

The Wicked Witch's Rules

Rule One: *Magic must have meaning to have power.* Above and beyond all else, this rule is the most important of all. If something doesn't make sense to you, if it doesn't evoke strong emotional responses, then you're just wasting time and going through the motions like a rote liturgy. Witches don't live that way, and they certainly don't weave magic that way.

Just because I write a book doesn't make me the spiritual expert for YOUR life, nor does it make me right a hundred percent of the time (ah, don't I wish!). So as you read, bear in mind that witchery is a very personal art. My guidelines and suggestions won't always work perfectly in your nine-to-five world. Please adapt and tweak the information here (and in any book of magic) so it better suits your vision and reality.

Rule Two: *Be your own priest, priestess, guru and guide.* Modern witches understand that in following a meaningful path this particular calling is ours alone to bear. Responsibility and accountability are among the things that remain foremost in an ethical witch's mind. We want to remain responsible for our powers and gifts, and accountable for how we use them, or a great deal of our magic loses meaning (refer to rule one above).

Understanding what we do and why we do it affects our witchery dramatically because understanding is a function of will. In becoming your own guide and guru, you open yourself up to possibilities and potentials, and will yourself to see more than surface reality. These possibilities and potentials include the periodic discovery that our intentions or tacks were incorrect, thus we return to being responsible and fixing any messes we make!

Rule Three: *Progress in witchery is* YOUR *progress, paced according to your vision.* It's fine to listen to well-intentioned advice on how to master certain processes, especially from people you trust and respect. Balancing that statement, you must decide what to accept or reject of this advice as effective and true for your spiritual life. So, if anyone suddenly becomes your personal magic critic, saying your way is wrong, tedious or too simple, then they obviously don't understand witchcraft at all. It is an art, and you are the artist!

When such moments arise (and trust me when I say they will), this is the perfect opportunity to put on your best wicked-witchy face, look very stern and politely tell him or her to butt out. A strong backbone is among the magickal practitioner's greatest tools. If you cannot stand up for what you believe, and what you know in your heart of hearts is best for you, then you cannot be a wicked witch. It's really that simple.

Rule Four: *Attitude is everything.* If your demeanor screams things like "naive" or "perpetual victim," you can bet that every mystical buzzard in the area will descend to try to feed off that energy. In magic and in life, like attracts like. So when your disposition bears dejected, uncertain, defeatist or other similarly negative vibes, it only makes matters worse.

It's often hard to shake bad feelings. You wouldn't be human if that weren't true. Wicked witchery doesn't advocate ignoring the fact that you feel lousy. Instead, it advocates adapting a different outlook, wrapping determination around your waist, getting off your beautiful, magical butt and doing something about it! This action alone will often change your attitude enough to get people to back off and let you work things out. It will also provide you with more positive energy.

Rule Five: *Even if you don't feel good, LOOK good, and always accessorize!* This rule has a lot in common with Rule Three. We unfortunately live in a very superficial society, so appearances can mean a lot. From a magical perspective, your appearance communicates specific energies, emotions and motivations to your environment. And there's nothing that irritates rivals or naysayers more than seeing someone they're trying to undermine looking as fresh as a daisy and filled with optimism.

Note here that I mean striking—not beautiful, not

handsome, but striking. Spiritually speaking, looking good is more a matter of carriage and demeanor than it is makeup, fashion sense and hairstyle. This is where your practice in glamoury will come in quite handy, as will your choice of magically enhanced baubles. By using these in tandem, you can project a specific image that sparkles with mystery, magic and witchery!

Rule Six: *Practice sound spiritual hygiene.* To my thinking, a witch has to be a good astral housekeeper. Just as a priest or priestess would tend a temple, we ARE our temples. By using spiritually sound purifying methods, we effectively shake off a lot of the unproductive dirt and debris that daily living leaves in our aura. We can also extend this idea to our homes and everything therein.

How? One witch might smudge his or her aura and home with sage and cedar incense to smoke out any lingering negativity. Another person might bathe himself or herself, and all magical tools, in lemon water for cleansing and purification. Still another practitioner might visualize a pure white, sparkling light filling every corner of his or her reality. What's important here isn't the method, it's taking the time to do it regularly.

How often? you may ask. As often as necessary to keep sticky, icky and otherwise nasty vibrations out of your aura. For people living in urban environments, I recommend doing this at least once a week. If you're fortunate enough to live in the country, you may have to do this only once a month, or after specific events that turn the energy patterns of your home or life topsy-turvy.

When you don't tend to spiritual housekeeping, you end up leaving stray energy all over the place: bits of anger, sadness, frustration, worry, pain and the like. These pockets of energy become emotional booby traps just waiting for psychically insensitive folks to wander in. Then what happens? Someone who was having a perfectly good day suddenly feels rotten.

On the other hand, when you're conscientious about spiritual hygiene, the results are astounding. You'll feel better (and I suspect everyone around you will too). You'll also find you're carrying far less tension throughout the day, so all your magical and mundane ventures flow more effortlessly.

Rule Seven: *Do unto others before they do unto you.* This doesn't mean that you should go looking for problems where none exist, or seek to purposefully harm people with your witchery. Instead it means living proactively. Set up magical and psychic protection for yourself and reinforce that protection regularly. Think ahead, then weave your magic accordingly so it reaches forward, patterning the future in the most positive way possible.

Along the same lines, constantly send out magic that supports your goals. Follow up that magic in word and deed, and LIVE THE MAGIC every moment of every day. If you do, your life cannot help but be transformed for the better.

Rule Eight: *Keep your nails and your wit sharp.* While wicked witches won't overtly scratch anyone's eyes out, there's no rule that says you can't *think* about it. Thoughts have power, but unless you act upon them these kinds of musings are pretty harmless and often release just the right amount of tension.

As for a keen wit, well, that's at the heart and soul of what it is to be a wicked witch. Learn to laugh at life and its odd twists. Learn to laugh at yourself when the moment calls for it. A good sense of humor is nothing less than essential if you're going to walk this path successfully. It's a coping mechanism, a source of energy, good soul food and a pretty good construct to use in spellcraft besides. Why? Because laughter indicates a strong emotional connection to what you're doing. In turn, the connection and the power released by laughter help you manifest your magic.

Rule Nine: *Living well is the best revenge.* Want to know the secret of getting even magically and mundanely? This is it! The sweet savor of success when looking in the eyes of an old rival or enemy is nothing less than wonderful.

Better still, if you designed your witchcraft in such a way as to harm no one, you have the satisfaction of knowing you achieved this victory without stepping on the little guy in the process. Wicked witches always side with the little guys, because we're often one of them.

Rule Ten: *Own a decent broom.* While your BMW might be better transportation, brooms symbolically sweep out the dirt in life, and sweep in good luck. If that doesn't work, you can always use it to chase annoying children or guests out of the house. When there's no broom around, try a Dustbuster instead and suck up that negativity.

Rule Eleven: *Learn the lingo.* Walking the walk is important, but so is talking the talk. In witchy circles we need to be aware of our communications. There is a huge difference between knowing our art and bragging about it or demeaning those who don't fully understand our craft. On the other hand, wicked witches aren't prone to mincing words when the need arises. The key is knowing what to say and when to say it (and also knowing when it's best to hold your tongue).

When all else fails, laugh . . . cackle loudly at life and its odd twists and turns. The sound of heartfelt laughter is guaranteed to send any negativity, bad vibes and snitty people running for the hills.

Rule Twelve: *The worse it sounds or looks, the better it works.* This seems especially true in food magic for some reason. For example, I made cream of brussels sprouts soup to smooth the way for prosperity once—it looked like green plaster, but it tasted great, and money started rolling in a few days later! This illustration aside, the old spell books often included terrible-sounding stuff, probably to scare off the uninitiated. So, in keeping with our wicked attitude and demeanor, go ahead and play a little with your magic. If you want, make a code in your spell book (like worms equaling noodles). It will certainly be fun and confound any stray eyes that decide to go peeking in those pages without permission!

Rule Thirteen: *Don't turn people into toads.* This kind of thing is very passé and uncreative (not to mention the three-fold case of warts that go with it karmically). More seriously, make every effort to keep your magick focused on the positives. In the long run, you'll benefit far more than by taking a darker path.

Rule Fourteen: *Admit when you screw up; celebrate when you do it right.* Modesty is a good attribute for any witch to cultivate. It helps us recognize both our strengths and weaknesses so we can accent the good and work on the bad. Since working on the bad is a huge part of wicked witchery, we have to be willing to concede errors humbly (i.e., with as little pouting as possible). Conversely, when magic works right and our lives begin to manifest that "rightness," it is certainly cause for honest celebration. Pat yourself on the back, revel in that moment, be thankful, then move on, carrying the residual hope in your heart as a motivating force.

Rule Fifteen: *Keep everything in balance and have fun.* An experienced witch is one who knows that spirituality must have a place in our real lives in order to make the changes for which we hope. To accomplish this, we must also maintain the delicate balance between word and silence, mind and heart, thought and action, the temporal and magical. No one ever said that a wicked witch wasn't also a wise one!

Beyond balance, witchcraft is, above all else, fun. Wicked witchery in particular strives for spontaneity, good humor, playfulness and friskiness to keep life and magic from getting stale or boring. Believe me when I say you'll never meet a drab or unimaginative wicked witch, and that if you embark on this path you'll never run the risk of being called dull!

Finally, a personal motto that you may wish to adapt (or not) from my own book of magickal experience is this: Keep it simple and sublime (or KISS). We are all very busy these days, so keeping our efforts uncomplicated is often a necessity. Remember: As long as meaningfulness is present, simplicity does not result in feeble witchery. In fact, your magic will often manifest more powerfully because you can really focus on the process rather than a lengthy list of details. So pucker up!

⇥ two ⇤

Alchemy 101:
Mixin' Up the Magic

By the pricking of my thumb,
something wicked this way comes.
—Shakespeare

In the immortal words of the great bard: *Eye of newt, toe of frog, wool of bat and tongue of dog.* Yuck! That doesn't sound like anything on my grocery list, and you certainly won't find this stuff at the local twenty-four-hour store! So what's a respectable wicked witch to do? Where exactly does a person find decent spell, charm and ritual components these days?

The answer may surprise you, but please bear with me for a moment while I take the long road in replying. First, in keeping with the title of this chapter, I'd like to roll back the pages of time to share a brief glimpse of an ancient magical art called alchemy. With roots that reach as far back as ancient Egypt and possibly beyond, alchemy found its way into the practices and philosophies of Greece, Rome, Arabia and medieval Europe.

The ancient alchemists were a curious and optimistic lot. They hoped to gain mystical wisdom and material wealth by transmuting base metals into gold, curing all manner of illness and conferring youth. In the process, they figured they'd also gain insights into the universe's mysteries. The result of their search wasn't quite what they expected, but certainly worthwhile. The studies of math, physics, philosophy, medicine and astronomy all benefited substantially from the efforts. Wouldn't it be nifty if our magical pursuits had similar results? Well, they can!

Since an effective witch blends everyday life with his or her magic in powerful and personal ways, there's absolutely no reason we can't begin to affect our world (or at least our corner of it) for the better. In this case being "wicked" means having a wicked, persistent desire to transmute the negatives into positives. The study of alchemy was dedicated to this kind of transformative process, which is why it makes a good illustrative starting point for how a witch chooses his or her components, tools and processes.

The Alchemy of Wicked Witchery

Many alchemists were considered heretics, or, at a minimum, somewhat eccentric. To curious onlookers it seemed as if they were trying to imitate or re-create God's handiwork. The negative cloud under which alchemists often worked is one that witches seem to live beneath too—being misunderstood, misrepresented or mocked with winks and nods by their families, townspeople or society as a whole. The similarities between the two don't end there either.

In the alchemical view of life, there is a definite correspondence and connection between the tangible and spiritual worlds. This connection is one that the witch actively seeks out and strengthens. It also corresponds nicely to the witch's motto: "As within, so without; as above, so below!"

Second, in this philosophical system, all things are regarded as bearing a seed of the Divine. Trusting in this truth, alchemists hoped to find these seeds and harvest them wisely so as to literally transmute one type of vibrational energy into another and revolutionize reality. Emulating this bold alchemical spirit, witches seek to do likewise. In this case, our "seeds" equate to using the best ingredients and processes we can find so that our magic grows into fullness.

Third, alchemy was the mystical ancestor for modern chemistry, one that blended magical and spiritual ideals with sound, scientific experiments. Following suit, many wicked witches are pretty good at wearing another hat too—that of playing "mad scientist"! If you have a closet or room where you can start assembling the basics of your witchery, it's a really nice alchemical advantage. This, at last, brings me to the subject of exactly what witchy tools and components you'll want to place in this magical laboratory (bet you thought I forgot!).

Tools of the Trade

The alchemists tried to transmute lead into gold. This makes a rather lovely analogy for all witches to consider—even the most common and plain of things has magical potential if you're willing to look! Even so, it's highly unlikely that most of us can obtain laboratory equipment and hundreds of exotic components like our scientifically minded predecessors did. Instead, in a typically creative wicked-witchy (and budget-minded) way, we look for tools and ingredients that are around us everyday.

Just as a plumber carries various-size wrenches, most witches have a couple of tools that they prefer to use for specific magical undertakings. In considering our choice of implements, however, there's a bit of a problem. There is little, if anything, on this planet that cannot function perfectly well in the wicked witch's astral arsenal, be it old or new, natural or man-made. The trick here is choosing among all the possibilities.

Perhaps the best answer to this difficulty is returning to our KISS philosophy and the helpful hints left by our ancestors. Look to what you have already, consider the meaningfulness in those items and then determine which ones make the most sense under the circumstances. From this point forward, putting the witchery together is mostly a matter of willpower and tenacity.

Animals and Insects: The ancients used a variety of animal and insect parts in spells and rituals because (a) the creature was sacred to a specific god or goddess, (b) because it was a valuable offering or (c) because the creature's characteristics represented the energy desired. Modern witches, being an earth-friendly group, no longer go to such drastic measures just to empower a spell.

But what about the wicked witch's pot? Seems kind of wanting without something furry or slimy! Don't worry, you have a lot of alternatives. Witches believe that in a sacred setting a symbol is just as potent as what it represents. So rather than using a whole animal, collect a pet's shed whiskers and fur. Or take nature walks and watch for feathers, eggshells, bones, dead insects, et cetera. If an insect won't be harmed by the spell, you may gather a live one, then release it after the procedure to likewise release your magic. As still another alternative, use a picture or carving of an animal to energize the magic (like carrying a stone statue of a bear for strength).

Aromatics: Aroma is a sensual cue and a supportive element for witchery. The scent chosen always corresponds to the energy being created so as to charge the air with sympathetic vibrations (see also Witchy Aromatherapy in Chapter 1). So, it's not surprising to discover a wicked witch's aromatics are as spicy, savory, suggestive and energetic as our magic!

Athame: The traditional ritual knife of Wiccans, an athame might be used to cut ritual herbs or cakes, to inscribe emblems in the air, to point the way for energy to follow and the like. This tool represents the masculine powers of the universe and the two-edged nature of our craft. Needless to say, wicked witches like to keep ours sharp and pointy, like our wits and tongues!

Athames are usually made out of any metal other than iron (iron is sometimes considered antimagic). So, if you don't have a fancy dagger about, a butter, steak or penknife will do just fine. Some other potential applications for an athame in wicked witchery include separation rituals, spells for cutting away unwanted ties to a situation/person, visualizations for balancing your "good" witch against the "bad" witch and hexes for getting to the point.

Bell: While you won't see these in every Wiccan tradition, bells are handy tools that represent protection, announcements or news and the feminine force of creation (the womb shape). I personally like using a pleasant-sounding bell or prayer bowl to center and focus myself for meditation. Some people ring a bell in lieu of lighting candles at the four quarters (the directional points of a circle, each of which has elemental energies: north, earth; south, fire; west, water; and east, air).

Bells are also helpful in spellcraft where you can use them to signal the sending of magic along its way. For example, if attempting to get someone to call, I might go to the telephone with a handheld silver bell and say:

_____ [name of person],

Heed my words, and answer them well,

When thrice I ring this silver bell.

I would then ring the bell clearly three times and leave it near the phone to resonate with my wish to the person in question. Don't have a bell handy? Well, a nice-sounding pot will do, as will a glass if you hit it lightly with a piece of silverware!

Other good applications for bells in your wicked witchery include rituals that announce your intentions, message spells and as protective amulets (bells have strong associations with banishing unwanted energy).

Brazier: An antiquated word for a fire-safe container in which you burn things, a brazier is nearly indispensable in wicked witchery. Considering that our goals include banishing the dark clouds that hang over our lives, weeding out troublemakers and destroying negativity, fire is certainly a good choice of elements to aid in such matters. It is both a source of light and warmth, and a means of symbolically obliterating any evidence of those things we no longer need or want.

By way of example, say you were experiencing a streak of seemingly endless bad luck. To transmute this negative energy, you could put an item that represents bad luck into a burning brazier. As that token ignites and burns to ashes, you might add an incantation like: *"Misfortune burn! The tide's about to turn!"* For best results keep repeating the incantation until the fire goes out by itself. You can then bury or disperse the ashes to break apart the unconstructive energy. Note that the components for this spell were the paper, the fire and the incantation, but the *tool* is the brazier.

Church-styled braziers can be purchased at Catholic supply stores, but there are alternatives. Cone incense burners are often deep enough for self-burning charcoal, for example, and a fireplace will certainly work. Or get a stoneware bowl and fill it with dirt or sand. Put this on top of a trivet, then make a small nest in the center in which to ignite a small fire source.

Candles: Candles can represent the presence of the Divine and the elemental powers of creation in magical traditions, often being chosen for their color, shape or aromatic correspondences. Better still, candle magic is among the simplest and least expensive methods in any witch's repertoire. There are many ways of applying this tool, including: (a) walking the perimeter of your sacred space with a lit candle to welcome the guardians or banish negative energy; (b) lighting a candle at the four corners of your sacred space to symbolize the guardians and/or one in the center for the Sacred; (c) using floating candles in spells and rituals where you wish to blend the energies of water and fire together and (d) wielding a lit candle as an alternative wand or athame that really puts a fire under the magic.

In some instances, candles become more than just a tool; they are also a component in the magic, making them doubly serviceable. In fact, you can add them to nearly any magical process you have going. For example, carve the image of what you most need or desire into a candle, focusing on your goal. Try to pick a candle whose color represents that goal, and dab it with a sympathetic oil. Light the candle as part of a spell or ritual, adding an incantation if you wish, then let the candle burn until the symbol has melted out of it. Keep the wax to reuse for similarly themed spells.

Or warm a nondrip candle gently so it gets slightly soft. Do a touch test to make sure it's safe to handle, then mold it into a shape that represents something/someone you wish would "disappear." Burn this pseudopoppet (see page 66 for more on poppets) completely (since nondrip candles leave no wax behind, the image literally disappears, supporting the magic).

Cauldron: What's a cackling witch without an old-fashioned iron pot in which to stir up his or her magic? Shakespeare would roll over in his grave to discover that modern witches use everything from oven pots and blenders to simple bowls for this purpose. Yes, the traditional form of a cauldron was a large pot with three legs (representing the three-fold goddess, but more practically providing solid support). But except at occult shops and mail order suppliers, these aren't always easy to find.

The cauldron becomes a handy oversize bowl in which one may make potions, blend up sachets, bubble up magical soap and even prepare the post-ritual feast! The only word of caution here is that you should not prepare edible items in the same pot as incense, soap and other nonedibles. Some of the base components might linger in the pot and really taint the flavor of the food (or worse, make you sick).

Crystals, Metals and Minerals: The earth's bounty serves a wicked witch well. Crystals work wonderfully as part of portable magic (charms, amulets, et cetera) because they represent a specific kind of energy and can also store our magical power (quartz is great for this). Besides this, you can use stones in spells for grounding and soil blessing (putting the stone back into the earth), or detachment (you throw the object away afterward), or in wish magic (tossing the item into a well).

Exactly what stones, metals and minerals you choose for any type of magic will, of course, change with your intentions. Following is a brief list of some easily obtained crystals and metals, along with common magical correspondences to get you started. Please note that this is abbreviated at best. For more information, I suggest referring to a good book on the magic of crystals and metals like Sirona Knight's *Pocket Guide to Crystals and Gemstones* (Crossing Press, 1998).

Crystal, Metal and Mineral Correspondence List

Agate (green): blessing your magical garden

Agate (black and white): turning away the evil eye

Agate (brown): inspiring victory in battles of any kind

Agate (blue): attracting peace, friendship and love

Agate (red): banishing, anti-spite talisman

Amber: capturing what you most need or desire

Amethyst: negating depression, self-control

Beryl: ceasing gossip

Bloodstone: improving business skill, boldness

Brass: augmenting money magic, health

Carnelian: enhancing communication, erotic energy

Cat's Eye: supporting beauty glamoury, luck, sun magic

Copper: channeling energy where you want it to go

Coral: sustaining water magic, protection against all ills

Fluorite: motivating conscious awareness, clever-mindedness

Geodes: strengthening goddess-centered magic

Gold: harnessing the sun's masculine-oriented energies

Hematite: building sturdy foundations, grounding

Iron: protecting yourself from magical attacks, strength

Jade: nurturing love, prosperity, happiness (a "feel-good" stone)

Lapis: finding your path, spirituality

Lead: insuring the longevity of a project, divinatory ability

Lodestone: attracting what you wish/need

Moonstone: developing the psychic witch within, lunar magick

Quartz (clear): collecting and projecting energy

Quartz (pink): manifesting friendship and love (especially self-love)

Salt: cleansing and purification

Silver: discovering the intuitive self, dream work

Tin: improving good fortune

Turquoise: refilling the inner well, safe travel

It's an interesting aside to note that a wicked witch's wand is often topped in, or made of, crystals and metals, denoting their connection to both the spiritual world and the earth.

Divination Tools: Among the many things necessary to effective wicked witchery is a good sense of foresight. The whole idea is to stay alert and aware enough to magically offset potential problems before they arise, or at least find a witchy coping mechanism when the proverbial s--t has already hit the fan. Both of these conditions are exactly the functions for which divination tools were designed.

In Chapter 3, I'll be providing you with some good examples of both traditional and adaptive divination methods. The key here is to find one approach that makes sense to you and works regularly, no matter where you find yourself.

Earth/Soil: Let's get dirty! Witches love to work directly with an element whenever possible, as it attunes our spirits and really improves results (see also Elemental Items, below). Soil is an excellent example. In the rich womb of the Mother we can plant our magic and help it grow (seeds are good for this), or bury those things that are better left behind (anything biodegradable works to break down the energy).

By the way, whenever there's a lot of "BS" going on in your life, try releasing it back to the earth's soils. The Mother knows how to handle dirt in all its forms. Better still, She makes something wonderful out of it (just look at composting!).

Elemental Items: In neo-Pagan traditions, the elements of earth, air, fire and water are believed to be part of all things. Nonetheless, each item and person on the planet has a specific element to which it is most strongly attuned. A seashell, for example, is under water's dominion because that is where the shell spends most of its existence—in the earth's watery womb.

In the witch's bag of tricks, elemental items are nearly essential because they represent the forces of all creation. Many witches keep small elemental tokens on their altar or at the four points of the sacred circle (page 52) to honor and welcome these forces into magical processes. For specific examples of the ways in which the elements participate in modern magic, see Earth/Soil (page 59), Wind/Air (page 68), Water/Rain/Ice/Snow (page 67) and Fire (below).

Fire: We talked a bit about the fire element with braziers earlier this chapter. Witches use fire to mark a gathering place for rituals because it lights up the night, just as we illuminate our minds and spirits with magic. Beyond this, however, fire is an important component in many spells and rituals. You can burn your wishes in a fire to release them, you can cleanse an area with smoke from a sacred fire and you can scry (divine) by fire, just to name a few.

For wicked witchery specifically, I recommend using fire as a motivating force ("put a fire under it"), as part of love/romance magic (symbolizing warmth and passion, but keep this fire controlled so it doesn't burn out), as a purgative (burn away what you do not need or want) and as a destructive force (to reduce negativity to ashes).

Flowers, Trees, Herbs and Other Plants: I'd hazard a guess that there's nothing on this planet that hasn't been used at least once as a magical component. All forms of plant life find their way into witchy potions, incense, charms, smudge sticks, medicine bundles, edibles, anointing oils and potpourris, and that's just the beginning! So for the green-thumbed witch reading this, or those with ready access to plant life, it's a great source of symbolism for nearly any magical need or process.

Flower, Tree and Herb Correspondence List

Alfalfa	safety, abundance, providence
Aloe	glamoury, good fortune, health
Anise	working with spirits, communication
Apple	health, knowledge, faithfulness
Banana	god magic, fertility (all kinds)
Basil	divination, love, protection
Bay	vitality, spirituality, well-being
Beans	sexual prowess (male), divination
Celery	balance, lucidity, clear thoughts
Cinnamon	power, passion, zeal
Clover	hex breaking, luck, banishing gainsayers
Daisy	sun magic, predictive powers, alertness

Dandelion	message spells, reading signs and omens
Elm	fairy magic, turning away unwanted desire
Garlic	exorcism, banishing psychic or mental vampires
Ginger	success, increased energy, daring efforts
Grape	festivity, fertility, pampering
Lemon	romance, longevity, pucker power (for kissing up when necessary)
Mint	money, sexual energy, healing, relaxation
Oak	safety, abundance, luck, making opportunities
Onion	turning away negativity, visions, healing emotional bumps and bruises
Peach	wish magic, sagacity
Pine	anti-magic, protection, purification
Rose	blessing, romance, intuitive-receptive sense
Sage	purification, wishcraft, keeping away people who bug you

Sunflower	sun magic, opening yourself
Vanilla	power, awareness, relationships, clarity
Walnut	conscious mind, cleverness

It's impossible in a book of this nature to provide you with all the natural correspondences that exist. Consequently, this list is very limited, but you can find more detailed information in Paul Beryl's *Herbal Magick* (Phoenix), my book *The Herbal Arts* and other similar books.

Goblet: Another portrait of the goddess, a goblet holds the ritual beverage (sometimes a potion), some of which is often given by way of libation to the earth or the Divine, and the rest of which is shared by participants. For those who may not have a chalice, or prefer something sturdier, your favorite coffee cup will certainly fit the bill. Wicked witches are amazingly pragmatic and laid back on this issue. If it's handy and bears the right symbolic value, go for it!

God/dess Images: Many witches choose to follow a specific god or goddess. For wicked witches, Hecate seems to be among the favorites. So, they might honor that Being by keeping a statue, painting, carving or whatever in a special spot often surrounded by flowers, plants or stones sacred to that power. This location then becomes central to many of the witch's efforts. For more information about gods and goddesses, I recommend Michael Jordan's *Encyclopedia of Gods.*

Hair, Fingernails and Body Fluids: Ah, now we're getting to something that sounds "wicked"! And truthfully, hair, fingernails and body fluids were often used for rather unseemly purposes in the past. The modern wicked witch is a little wiser. Rather than applying these things to curse or harm, we use them as a power boost that bears a strong personal signature. Just as an animal's scent marks its territory, a witch's hair, fingernails, tears, saliva and urine can be a potent and poignant maker's mark!

I know some people get a little antsy thinking about using urine in magic, but it's been a common component in witch bottles (see Chapter 5) for quite some time. The acidic nature makes it a great protective ingredient. For men, it's doubly useful because they can literally pattern the magic they wish to create by drawing a symbol.

As for applying the rest: Use hair in rituals that focus on difficult situations (where you're "pulling your hair out"), in spells aimed at improving strength (note Samson) and in beauty glamouries (perhaps as a portable charm to augment). Use fingernails when you wish to alleviate annoyances ("fingernails on the chalkboard"), to magically handle something that's been itching at you, when you need to dig in or hang on or to help in making a point. Tears are excellent in forgiveness spells, and saliva is traditionally used for healing and protection.

Household Items: In times past, witches lived in a small village (or just outside of town), and pretty much had to depend on what they had, could grow or could trade for in terms of components. So, in blending up potions, you'd find them using a pot and wooden spoon, for example, because they were both handy and functional.

In keeping with this tradition, the modern witch often turns to common household items as components in his or her magic. For example, I like to use glue for tenacity spells (so I "stick" to it), matches in power pouches for passion (so I can light my "fire"), spoons and bowls in rituals for returning negativity to its source (literally "dishing it out") and so forth. These examples are illustrations of pun magic, and how the simplest items can be marvelously potent for our witchery if we can see past commercialism and focus on potential.

Incense: In applying various ingredients for a specific goal, incense makes a great medium through which to express our witchery. Here you can blend all kinds of charged herbs, spices, aromatic woods, et cetera into something symbolically potent and personally pleasing. My only caution is this: Don't put too many ingredients into your incense.

Generally two to three well-chosen components for your incense will do a much better job than a dozen most times. Why? Going back to KISS, the clarity of a component's energy is maintained more precisely when only a few ingredients are present. And, in more complicated blends, you can't always be sure you've balanced the aroma (which also represents the vibration of the blend) in such a manner that it's pleasing until after you've already burned it.

Poppets: Poppets are little dolls made out of personal clothing and stuffed with herbs or other plant matter that represents the magic at hand. Some people use a carved lemon, a potato, shaped clay and other malleable substances instead, and all of these options are perfectly suited to creative witchery.

While the wicked witch might want to "voodoo unto others" through the use of a poppet, most witches feel it's prudent to use poppets only as self-help items, or with the permission of those we wish to help. As angry as I get, and as much as those pins get really tempting, I don't want to get stuck three-fold in return, so I have to agree here. Besides, since you can make poppets in any shape, including that of your home or a beloved pet, they're incredibly useful for sympathetic magic of any type!

Robes: In Chapter 1, we talked about dressing suitably for your role as a wicked witch. In some settings people choose a robe for this job because it evokes that wonderful old-world feeling. Magic has a timeless appeal, and putting on a robe certainly helps me get in the mood (not to mention that it's really comfortable). This isn't a necessary tool, but it's one worth considering if you find you're having trouble switching gears from everyday mundanity.

Techno Gadgets: In an effort to keep our magic from getting stale or meaningless, wicked witches are always thinking about how they can use the newfangled goodies that technology is forever providing to us. You'll see examples of this throughout these pages, but just to note a few: The microwave can quicken a spell's manifestation (we already use it to speed up food preparation), the computer can be used for networking magic and the (inactive) TV screen is a suitable scrying (divination) surface!

Wand: Think of a wand as a pointer on the universe's chalkboard and you'll understand this tool's use very well. Any long item with a distinctive end can become a wand for directing your magical power more specifically (yes, I do mean anything, from a wooden spoon to your pointer finger). As long as it's meaningful and treated respectfully, it will work.

Witches sometimes use a wand to draw sacred emblems in the air or on the ground. In this case the wand takes on the function of an astral pen or paintbrush, applying energy where it's most needed.

Water/Rain/Ice/Snow: Of all the elements, I like working with this one the best because it has so many forms and possibilities. Moving water, such as streams (or a garden hose), is a medium for carrying our magic toward its goal, or away from something/someone. Dancing in the rain is a great way to connect with the water element and its energies, not to mention your inner child. Ice was among the first components used for binding and protecting magic. Snow has magical potential because you can shape it and let it melt (dispersing or diminishing the energy of the shape created), and steam is a neat way to mix the energies of earth and air together.

Wind/Air: I've spoken already about the importance of the elements in magic. What's wonderful about the wind is that it moves from various directions, each of which can represent one elemental component when its physical manifestation isn't available. Specifically, the north wind is earth, the east wind is air, the southern wind is fire and the western wind becomes water. These correspondences sometimes vary from tradition to tradition, but these are the most globally recognized in mystical practices.

Also, each wind bears the energy of its corresponding element, so standing in a specific wind during a ritual, or casting components into the winds, can give the spell unique qualities. Use a north wind for foundation and grounding; an east wind for hope, new beginnings and communication; a south wind for love, passion and energy; and the west wind for healing, peace and intuitive matters.

You: It amazes me how many witches forget about the tool and component they have with them all the time. WE are the magic, and we are the most important component in any spell or ritual. You can do without the tools. You can move past using ingredients. As long as you have a strong will and keen focus, you've got everything you need for your wicked witchery in your back pocket already.

Processes

In the chapters that follow, we will be discussing the specifics of finding and using divination tools, making amulets, charms and talismans, of creating or adapting spells and brewing potions. Each of these aspects is a time-honored technique that's very common to all forms of witchery. They are, effectively, core methods that you'll see throughout the world's magical traditions and writings.

I've chosen to focus on these core methods in this book for several reasons. First, they follow the wicked witch's axiom: If it ain't broke, don't fix it! These techniques have successfully served wizards and cunning folk for thousands of years. I see no reason they shouldn't continue so doing.

Second, the power of tradition is strong and enduring. Think of any belief or practice that's been held in the communal mind and heart for hundreds of years, and the kind of energy this produces. A clever witch uses tradition as an energy well, adding creative personalization as a guiding force for applying that tradition.

Third, I have always considered it a witch's duty to honor and pass along our history to future generations. The magical arts are very, very old, but what most people know of them is often skewed or just plain wrong. Holding true to the basics of our heritage allows us to pass on that richness to our children. They, in turn, can take magic into the future with less fear and more power.

Augmenting Processes

It's the success, longevity and positive energy in traditional magickal processes that makes them important to wicked witchery. But what other customary amplifications can be used in conjunction with these to improve your results? You actually have a lot from which to choose, which I'll cover in a minute. Just remember in reading this section that, for wicked witches especially, more does not equal better! One amplification, carefully considered and sensitively added to a magical process, can be far more effective than adding several.

Ambience: Call this "mood magic"! The ambience in which you work your witchery can make a big difference to the outcome, especially for urban-dwelling witches. Straighten up the area in which you're working (to improve the flow of *chi*, a universally positive energy), light some candles, burn a favored incense, play some New Age music and turn off the outside world for a moment. Always match these adjustments to the theme of your magic. For example, if you're feeling naughty, go with black candles that correspond to your mood. No matter your choices, actions like these become a mini-ritual that readjusts your mental processes and prepares the way for magic.

In creating a magickal ambience, don't forget to provide yourself with sensual cues. Each sense (hearing, vision, touch, taste and smell) confers specific signals to your mind on a conscious or subconscious level. For example, think of the reaction you have to the smell of fresh-baked bread or cookies. You don't consciously make an effort to have that reaction, it just happens naturally. Well, you can invoke similar effects supernaturally by giving yourself more sensual input throughout the magical method at hand.

If you have to choose among the senses, try to appeal to the one that inspires you the most. For example, I'm very tactile and will often pick the fabric in my robes to match the mood of my magic. On the other hand, each sense that you involve in your magic will improve the outcome geometrically, so add as many as you can in creative and meaningful ways.

Sacred Space: Consider enacting your magical processes in the protected confines of a sacred space. More than simply being a safe haven, the sacred space develops, nurtures and holds your magical energy in place until you're ready to release it. The sacred space also marks a definitive line between world and not-world, something very important to the overall productivity of your spiritual time. It's hard to get witchy when you're thinking about everything *but* magic!

Every magical tradition has a different way of creating sacred space. For the wicked witch, it might be fun to set up the magical workroom in a halloween-ish style with a broom for the air/east quarter, a cauldron for the water/west quarter, a frog image for the north/earth quarter, a fire source in the south with incense burning and maybe some dry ice in the center for Spirit (the resulting fog creates a very magical, otherworld feeling). This isn't necessary, but it's certainly fun, and sets the tone for wicked witchery nicely.

Here's one potential invocation to use if you've set up the sacred space as described herein.

East   *Sweep in the new, sweep out the old*
              Now the magic shall unfold!

South   *Fire, fire burning bright,*
              Light the darkness, reclaim the night!

West   *Cauldron burn, cauldron bubble,*
              By my words the magic doubles!

North   *Jump, frog, jump, bring the earth's power up!*
              Leap, leap! Through this space let magic seep!

Center   *Power release, power roll; as above, so below!*
              Magic round like this fog spins, as without,
                       so within!

As you can see, the speaker of the invocation "invites" the power of each quarter in a clockwise progression to encourage positive energy. Dismantling sacred space usually proceeds counterclockwise. As with all forms of witchery, this may vary by tradition and the magical theme. Banishing circles (ones intended to rid the practitioner[s] of specific energies), for example, are often invoked counterclockwise to correspond with the desired outcome.

Timing: Any time is the right time for magic, but when you want to add another dimension to your craft, timing is certainly a good choice. The ancient magickal practitioners wholly trusted in the saying: "As above, so below." Consequently, they often timed their spells, rituals and other magical procedures so they coincided with specific moon phases and other propitious astrological configurations.

To apply this outlook, there are two problems that stand in a wicked witch's way: (a) a schedule that doesn't often allow for flexibility or free time at the right moment; and (b) not knowing what moon phase, moon sign, month, day and hour correspondences exist, or when each occurs. While months and days might be easy, seeing the moon in the city is not! The easiest way to solve this problem is by getting a good astrological calendar (Llewellyn produces one annually) so you can check the favorable upcoming aspects as compared with your schedule.

In the meantime, you can use these guides as a general reference:

Moon Phases

- **Waxing moon:** supports magic for growth, progress, travel, advancement, breakthroughs and improved luck.
- **Full moon:** supports magic for maturity, insight, the psychic self, fulfillment, fertility, abundance and prosperity.
- **Waning moon:** supports magic aimed at ban-

ishing, decreasing, deterring stress, expelling negativity and generally turning things in a different direction.

- **Dark moon:** supports magic aimed at rest, dream work, leisure, weeding out the garden of our lives and introspection (meditation).

Weekdays

- **Monday:** magick focused on the intuitive, lunar nature. Also good for spiritual progress, creativity and abundance.

- **Tuesday:** magick focused on the rational mind. Also good for improving personal skills, handling legal matters and physical fitness.

- **Wednesday:** magick focused on inventiveness and whimsy. Also good for developing humor, clever tacks and psychism.

- **Thursday:** magick focused on strength and power. Also good for stressing devotion, persistence and tenacity.

- **Friday:** magick focused on interpersonal relationships of any type, especially love. Also good for manifesting good communication skills, proficiency and productivity.

- **Saturday:** magick focused on transformation and motivation. Also good for comprehension and personal maturity.

- **Sunday:** magick focused on the conscious, solar self. Also good for improving mental keenness, logic, strength and courage.

Months

- **January:** safety and watchfulness
- **February:** well-being, forgiveness and poise
- **March:** success, adeptness and vanquishing shadows
- **April:** good luck, opportunities and beginnings
- **May:** development, fertility and enrichment
- **June:** dedication, loyalty and constancy
- **July:** self-regulation, dignity and courage
- **August:** peace, harmony and unity
- **September:** spirituality and comprehension
- **October:** maturity, change and revolution
- **November:** intuitiveness, kindness and universal balance
- **December:** awareness, keen discretion and frugality

Since putting all this information together for spellcraft and ritual can easily become very cumbersome, I usually rely on the moon phases. After all, each one comes at least once a month, so it's very accessible. Plus the moon phase fills the entirety of the day and night, so it's far more accommodating even with modern constraints.

Personalizing Your Art

Being a wicked witch, or a magician of any sort, is an art. This means that it will take time for you to develop your personal witchy "voice" or style to the level at which your tools and components come together in just the right way. At this point every word and action involved in your witchery bears immense meaning and power, and is personally fulfilling. But I can tell you from experience that there's no "instant" adeptness in this (or any) magical methodology, and that sometimes the road by which we arrive at our goals is as important, if not more so, than the goal itself.

Along the path to accomplishment you're likely to find one or two methods here that you personally enjoy more than the rest, and that seem most suited to your path and vision. This is terrific, and the way it should be. The nature of witchery encourages you to seek out things that give you pleasure and a sense of confidence in your magic. Keep this target in mind, and you'll rarely go wrong.

⋨ three ⋩

Witchy Vision:
Fortune-telling Made Easy

*The future cannot be hidden or obscured
from the intelligent soul.*
—Nostradamus

Y ou know, if more witches devel-
oped their psychic skills, specifically future-telling, we
could avoid a lot of the stuff that gets us into trouble.
The problem is that (a) most of us don't believe we have
any psychic aptitude; or (b) we don't pay attention when
those instincts make themselves known. This is a trend
that the wicked witch has to break if he or she is going to
live a truly enchanted life.

This chapter, therefore, introduces you to some easily
learned divination techniques. Each of the methods cov-

ered includes example applications specific to the questions that often come up in magick and daily life.

I've given these illustrations for several reasons. First, it helps show you what kinds of questions are suited to various divinatory mediums so you can formulate your own questions accordingly (and by so doing experience greater success).

Second, many people still think of fortune-telling as some kind of circus sideshow. The words "diviner" and "psychic" continue to conjure up images of a gypsy charging exorbitant amounts of money to answer questions about who a person will marry, or to seek messages from a dead relative. This portrait has little in common with the way contemporary diviners and divination systems work.

Wicked witches in particular usually have other things on their minds for supernatural information-gathering efforts than just talking to ghosts. Believing that "forewarned is forearmed," we try to weed out troublemakers, avoid nonproductive situations or relationships, improve our insights about problems that currently exist and dodge problems that haven't occurred yet! This way we can make the best choices possible given the circumstances at hand to smooth out the present and build a better future.

Personal and Environmental Arrangements

Before embarking on this type of astral excursion, it's a good idea to do some groundwork. Chapter 1 talked about extending your senses and using the input received from them as a mystical cue for coping with, reacting to and thinking about life. This ability is also very useful in divination, so practice it regularly before trying to use fortune-telling tools. This way your psychic sensitivity will be primed and ready for the task at hand.

Beyond honing your intuitive ability, you also have to be ready mentally, physically and spiritually for divination efforts. Don't pose questions about yourself or read for others when you're exhausted, depressed, frustrated, sick, angry or apathetic. Hey, even wicked witches have "off" days, and these kinds of conditions make for a very unproductive session.

Spiritual preparation requires a little more mental and physical preparation because different witches use different methods, depending on what works best for them. Here's a list of some common techniques for you to try. I'd suggest giving each a chance so you can find one or two that effectively center and focus your spirit:

- **Meditation:** To center yourself, get rid of excess tensions and heighten personal awareness (ten to fifteen minutes is suggested). Generally it's suggested that you sit with your back straight (the backbone carries mental, physical and spiritual signals throughout your body). However, if you find sitting like this distracts you too much, find a position in which you can be comfortable. Meditation won't help much if you feel itchy, wiggly or awkward.

After finding a physical posture that works for you, close your eyes. Breathe deeply using deep, all-connected breaths to relax, release tension and improve the overall meditative state. You may find you feel a little fuzzy, tingly or sense a slight buzzing. If so, you're doing it right!

- **Prayer:** To invoke the assistance of your patron/ness so that He or She guides your insights. Note that prayer need not be fancy, nor sound like King James's poetry. It also requires no particular posturing. Prayerfulness is determined by attitude—it is the intimate speaking of the soul to the god/dess. Use words with which you're comfortable and that express your needs/desires.

- **Sensory Cues:** To custom-design an atmosphere that tugs at your senses, drawing them to a higher level. Candlelight, incense, music, magical munchies (foods charged with energy or that have symbolic value, like cookies as a blessed comfort food) and special decorations are all examples of sensory cues.

- **Ceremonial Elements:** To signal your superconscious mind about the task at hand so that the reading proceeds sensitively and insightfully. Ceremonial elements include invocations, washing one's hands before taking out the divination tool, unwrapping or unboxing the divination tool in the same way every time, sitting in the same location for every reading and the like.

- **Warding**: To create a protected space in which your reading can flow without temporal or metaphysical interference. If you're not already familiar with creating a magick circle, refer to Chapter 2, Augmenting Processes, of this book.

- **Magical Augmentation**: To attract the best energies into the space where a reading takes place. Examples of effective magical aids include placing sympathetic crystals around the area (or table), carrying a divinatory charm or talisman, dabbing your third eye with psychically charged oils (rose is one option that many practitioners recommend) and smudging the area with sage or cedar smoke to dissipate any random energies that might hinder the reading.

In many instances, your environmental preparations key directly into the spiritual ones you've decided upon (namely, having all the tools/components you need in place). Besides these, you can also take some very simple precautions on a mundane level that will help your efforts greatly. Turn off the phone, put up a "Do Not Disturb" sign, ask housemates to respect your privacy and perhaps keep pets or children in another room. This way you can turn your attention directly to Spirit without interruptions that could get the reading off track.

The Right Tool for the Right Job

Step two for the gypsy-witch is finding a tool that functions well. Every person responds to divinatory tools differently. Some people find they like Tarot decks, while others feel the symbolism is too complex. Some enjoy pendulum work, while others just get cramped arms. So how do you figure out which systems have the greatest potential to appease your witchy vision and answer the question at hand?

First, trust your senses. If you're a highly visual person who likes more literal symbolism, you'll want a highly visual divination system with easily recognizable interpretive values! If you respond to tactile input, you'll want a textural system like runes or crystals, and if you respond positively to metaphorical input, you'll want to consider more figurative systems like ink blots and wax drippings.

Next, consider the kind of questions you're likely to ask of a divinatory tool. This will help you narrow the field of options considerably. For example, I suspect that most wicked witches are looking for nitty-gritty details, not simple yes or no answers. So binary systems like flipping a coin probably won't fulfill your requirements. Realistically, any system can provide you with binary responses with little, if any, alteration. Consequently, I suggest considering systems that offer a minimum of thirteen different symbols with which to work. Thirteen is the number of lunar cycles in the year, and the moon represents our spiritual, intuitive nature.

Windows into Time

Who of us isn't interested in gazing into the future, or at least looking at the present with a different perspective? For the wicked witch in particular, divination is a means to an end. In those moments when we can't seem to find the right attitudes or answers for living proactively and positively, divination becomes a very helpful technique. Divination tools access the psychic within, removing any blinders that hinder us from seeing what is often right in front of us. Additionally, divinatory mediums assist us in opening insightful windows, through which we can gather the information and outlooks we most need.

Since you're probably itching to get started, this section will focus wholly on divinatory tools that come from objects found in and around the sacred space of home. This is great for the budget-minded wicked witch who wants to hone and apply his or her psychic senses without having to spend a fortune. Also, since these objects come from your personal environment they already bear your alchemical energy signature, meaning they'll work more accurately!

Card Systems

Divination by cards is technically known as cartomancy. Thanks to New Age publishers, many people are already familiar with Tarot decks, but these can be very costly. And since you can't always see the whole deck before buying it, you may not even like all the symbols it offers. By way of a solution to this problem, this frugal (read: cheap) wicked witch came up with alternatives for you to try.

The Coupon Tarot: If your household is anything like mine, you probably get tons of these in the Sunday paper and the mail. They bear all kinds of pictures and words carefully chosen by advertisers to motivate a buyer. We can use this motivating power as a helpmate for divination.

To make this system, you'll first need to pick out at least thirteen different coupons of the same size, whose product names or imagery are different enough to represent a variety of human experiences. For example, a coupon bearing the image of Joy dish detergent can symbolize personal happiness, joyful occasions, et cetera. A coupon for baby products might be interpreted as a new beginning or a gestational project that needs attending. And a coupon for toothpaste might equate to matters of communication (especially those that need to be cleaned up!).

Once you've chosen your coupons, make notes of their meanings before you try a reading with them. Shuffle the coupons carefully so as not to tear them, then lay them out as you might any Tarot deck. A traditional three-card spread, for example, equates to the past, present and future of a specific situation/question (laying out the cards from left to right, left being the past, center the present and right the future).

Two other easy layouts are that of a single card pulled for a daily overview (this provides insights into your day), and a four-card, cross-shaped spread. This pattern frequently equates to the elements or directions, north being earth (or what the question is grounded in), east being air (what communications are happening with regard to the question), south being fire (what's heating things up or most energized) and west being water (what needs healing or more sensitivity).

Returning to the three-card spread, let's put all this into a functional illustration. Say you asked about a new project. In response you got the toothpaste coupon followed by the baby coupon and the dish detergent coupon. One possible interpretation is that you have to clear up communications with someone before this project will really get underway. If you do that, however, the results will be positive!

Note the results of your reading so you can meditate on it later. Afterward, pick out the coupons that represent the most positive outcome imaginable for your question. Put your palms facedown over these, visualizing your magic as white light that saturates the paper. Take these to the supermarket and use them to disperse their symbolic energy! If you'd rather that your coupon Tarot deck last a while, you can back them with some type of art board so they're sturdy and coat them with art spray for durability.

Greeting Card Tarot: The greeting card Tarot is based on a concept similar to the coupon Tarot, with a minor twist. In this case you'll want to collect same-size cards that you receive from well-wishers. The good feelings that inspired someone to give you the card will actually improve your readings thanks to the power of love and friendship! If you're feeling particularly impatient, you can *buy* the cards you want to use for your deck.

As with the coupons, you'll want a variety of imagery with which to work. Here are some common card covers and potential interpretations to get you started:

Candles: your hopes for the future

Car: movement, possibly travel

Cat: someone behaving cattily, or the need to regain your balance; alternatively, flexibility and cunning

Dog: devotion (or lack thereof) of a friend or loved one

Fairy: dreams and imaginings; just don't let these become so great a focus that you need a reality check

Flowers: an unexpected gift or news (note that the symbolism here can vary according to the type of flower, such as a red rose representing news from a loved one, and a yellow rose suggesting a gift from a friend)

Fruit: harvesting one's labors or deeds (as with flowers this can change according to the type of fruit, such as an apple representing the need to slow down at work so you don't get sick)

Hearts: literally, matters of the heart

House: focus on the home (or perhaps a new residence)

Noisemakers: be alert; possibly an upcoming celebration

Ribbons: personal ties and responsibilities

Star: a wish manifesting

Tree: strong foundations (change value by type of tree if desired, such as an oak indicating the need to support a newly initiated project or idea)

Let's put this cartomancy set to the test. Say you had a question about whether or not someone was trying to interfere in your relationship with a significant other. After focusing on this question and shuffling the cards, the answer comes up as an upright heart, the dog (upside down) and noisemakers (upside down). This, to me, says that there's a good chance you have a rival, and one who's gained undo attention, so be alert!

With this particular system the upright and reversed

images help give you more diversity to work with in interpreting your reading. So, you'll need to determine ahead of time what both posturings will mean in the finished deck. The simplest approach is simply reversing the meaning with the card's reversal. For example, while an upright heart portends good things for a relationship, a reversed heart could signify a falling out.

Finally, if you want to keep the cards for a long period of time, you may wish to back and coat them as you did the coupon deck.

Cast and Drawn Systems

While cards can be drawn out of a deck for abbreviated readings, they can't really be cast onto a surface like a crystal oracle or runes can. There are some advantages to the casting systems over drawn ones, specifically randomness. If you're working with different-size or -shape objects, it's easy to unconsciously hunt for the answer you want when drawing an item out of a bowl or bag. If casting them onto a cloth, however, this no longer becomes possible.

On the other hand, cast systems take longer to read (you use all the tokens and have to interpret them according to where they land). So, when time is tight, drawing out a symbol might be a wiser choice. In either case, the mediums I'm exploring here offer you *both* options. Choose the approach that suits your time constraints and the question being posed.

If you decide to draw out one or more tokens in

answer to your question, the interpretations should be pretty forthright. If you decide to cast them, draw a thirteen-inch circle on a cloth and use that for your surface. Anything that lands outside the circle isn't read. Objects to the left indicate negatives, to the right positives; at the top, things literally hanging over your head, and at the bottom, what's happening beneath the surface of this situation. Alternatively, things that land closer to you indicate more intimate matters and situations in the present, while those farther away speak of emotionally distant or future situations.

Junk Drawer: Go to your junk drawer and look at all the little items there: batteries, paper clips, tweezers, keys, string, et cetera. Each of these items has a specific significance that's based on how you use it in everyday life. The clever wicked witch takes this significance one step further and applies it to his or her divinatory efforts.

As before, you'll want to collect at least thirteen items that are small enough to fit inside a 4-by-4-inch pouch (like those from old Crown Royal bottles). As you pick these items, make a list and note their significance. Here's a list of things with potential interpretive values I found in my junk drawer:

Battery (AA): Watch your energy levels.

Business card (company name "Advantage"): A "go-ahead" signal—you have the advantage right now.

Chap Stick: A communication issue—are your words dry or insensitive toward someone you love?

Checker piece: It's your move in this situation.

Glue: If something's been broken or damaged, now's the time to fix it.

Key: An opening is being presented to you.

Label (blank): Watch yourself—you may be presuming incorrect information about something/someone.

Matches: Put a fire to something that you've gotten lazy or apathetic about.

Paper clip: Make connections, network.

Quarter: Someone's waiting for your call!

Rubber band: Be more flexible.

String: Tie up loose ends.

Wite-Out: Something's being hidden here. Be careful.

So, say you posed this question to the junk drawer medium: How can I advance myself at work without going against my professional scruples? When you cast the system onto a hand-drawn circle as instructed previously in this section, the Wite-Out landed at the bottom of the circle, the string at the top, the paper clip and key to the right and the label to the left. The interpretation here is that you've misread your current situation, and things may be worse than they seem. Someone is probably not being totally forthright, so tie up your loose ends at this job, do some protective magic and start networking. The good news is that the networking will bring sound leads and likely a much better job.

Nuts 'n Bolts: Nuts 'n bolts are tremendous fun for people who like working with tools. In this case, you'll be applying your "fix-it" knowledge for wicked witchery and gaining perspective while you work! Here's how.

Gather together small tools and pieces of hardware. You can use these in exactly the same way as the junk drawer mediums (casting or drawing them out). My only suggestion is that you check all the items for sharp or ragged edges that might cut you or tear through your casting/drawing bag. Carefully sand or tape those edges smooth as a safety precaution.

Here's a list of small tools and hardware that I found around my home and potential interpretive values to get you started:

Curtain fastener: Someone's peeking into your
life. Only you can decide if you want to leave
the curtains open!

Duct tape: Make sure your efforts are seamless; any oversights will come back to haunt you.

Electrical cap: Protect yourself; an onslaught of energy is coming your way.

Hook: What are you fishing for and do you have the right bait?

Instant adhesive: Someone or something has attached itself to you, for boon or bane.

Nail: Hammer home your point; don't mince words.

Plug (three-way): You'll need to tweak your connections for this situation to work effectively.

Refrigerator bulb: Shine a light on things and make sure to check for potential problems (note, this might be best suited to a drawn system due to its fragile nature).

Screw: Someone is putting it to you, and it's not fun.

Screwdriver (for eyeglasses): Are you using the right talents/tools for the task at hand?

Utility knife: Cut away what you don't need and get rid of it; simplify.

Wire: Security issues; something isn't as safe as you think.

Note that with things like the wire and duct tape you need not use the whole roll. Just take a snippet so that when you put them with your other mediums they will all fit into the storage space allowed.

For this method let's try this sample question: Should I stay in my current relationship? You shake up the bag and draw out the wire, utility knife and adhesive. This speaks loudly of an unproductive relationship that didn't have a lot of foundation upon which to build in the first place. One or the other of you is clinging out of a sense of fear or loneliness rather than really wanting to be a partner. Cut yourself free and move on!

The Toy Chest: Folks with children love this divinatory approach because it allows us to bring out the inner child and play a little under the handy guise of seeking wisdom (wicked witches *love* to play). As with the other systems discussed in this section, you're going to be looking for small objects suited for casting or drawing, and that have some obvious symbolism that you can easily apply to a divinatory effort.

I have three children of various ages. In looking through their toys, here's a sampling of what I found and potential interpretive values:

Car: Potential for movement, possibly travel.

Crayon: You already have the guidelines you need, now just "color" them in with your vision.

Dinosaur: Outmoded habits and ideas that hold you back are present.

Duplo or Lego: The need to build carefully.

Feather: Take a break and tickle your fancy!

I (Scrabble letter): You are either the problem or solution in this question.

Marble: The earth. You need to get back to nature and have some quiet time alone with the Mother.

Monkey: Stop monkeying around and get down to business!

Mini mailbox: A message is coming, so watch for it.

Piglet: Small things can be very important; pay attention.

Spoon: Don't dish it out if you're not willing to take it.

Table (doll house): Put your cards on the table confidently.

Wand: Time to put your wicked witchery to work!

The sample question this time will be: Why do I always seem to get involved with the wrong people? This question lays heavy on your heart for many days, and throughout that time you keep stumbling over the Scrabble letter "I" and crayons. This could be considered an omen or sign from the Universe that says, Stop being your own worst enemy. Look at what you have, work with it and make it the best it can be rather than living in the past.

Metaphorical Systems

I mentioned earlier in this chapter that some individuals may find metaphorical systems very useful. For those who have never tried to see pictures in clouds or ink blots, here are some helpful hints. First, don't try to look at a specific spot in the medium. Instead, let your vision blur a bit. Next, note your immediate impressions after your vision blurs. Even if you find later that you think you see something else in the pattern(s) created by the medium, your first impression is often the most instinctual—and witches know that magic and instinct go hand in hand.

Finally, look up the pattern in a book of dream imagery (like my *Language of Dreams*), a book that includes a variety of divinatory emblems (like my *Futuretelling*) or perhaps a book of emblems like Barbara Walker's *Woman's Dictionary of Symbols and Sacred Objects*. Books like these will give you a launching point for your interpretations. Add a healthy portion of personal insight to the process and you're likely to have very accurate results.

Beans: To try this medium you'll need a variety of beans: yellow, white, black, red, orange and green. Get enough to fill a spaghetti sauce–size glass jar with a secure lid (this way the thrifty witch can still use the beans for cooking). Hold the jar in your hand and close your eyes. Think about the question at hand and begin shaking the jar to mix the beans. Visualize as many details as you can about this situation (keep shaking).

Finally, open your eyes and look at the patterns created inside the jar. Or you can pour a handful of mixed beans onto a white surface like a cutting board instead. In either case you're looking for rough imagery to appear. For example, say someone asked why he or she was having problems with spellcraft. A pattern appeared that looked somewhat like an eye half-closed. This might be interpreted to mean that either this person wasn't opening themselves to psychic insights for magic, or that perhaps they weren't looking objectively at their spellcraft to fix the problems.

To adapt this medium to a cast or drawn system, all you need do is put an equal number of each bean in a bag and think of a question. Draw out a bean or cast the contents of the bag onto your circle, then interpret the results as follows:

Black: This is a negative response (or "stop").

Black-eyed: You need to focus and really keep your eyes open.

Brown: This indicates the need for grounding and foundations. Make sure you put your roots where they can grow the best.

Brown and white: Personal growth and enrichment is forthcoming.

Green: This is a positive response (or "go").

Orange: A friend can help you with this. Alternatively, cultivate a specific attribute to resolve things.

Red: Watch your energy levels and your temper.

White: Protect yourself and stay true to your ideals.

Yellow: Use creativity and effective communication to solve this situation.

Colored Rice: Rice is a symbol of good luck in the Far East, and a little extra luck is something of which every wicked witch could use more! To color white rice for divination, all you need do is soak it in food coloring and water briefly (I suggest a long-grain rice). It absorbs the color quite quickly. The nice part here is that you can dye rice in a wide variety of colors to increase interpretive values.

Lay the dyed rice out on several layers of paper towels to dry before using it as your fortune-telling medium. Once it's completely dry (usually twenty-four hours is a good amount of time), transfer the rice to a decorative clear bottle with a secure lid. This will keep the rice from getting sticky in humid weather, and allow you to use the bottle as an attractive magical knickknack when you're not divining with it.

To use the rice for scrying, follow the same procedure as that given for the beans (holding the bottle, thinking of your question, shaking the rice, then looking at the patterns). By the way, since you use food coloring to dye the rice, you can cook up a really positive reading and eat it to internalize the magic! Alternatively, you can sprinkle the rice on a preglued surface, then carry that paper as a charm/amulet to help attract positive energy for resolving the question/situation at hand. Just be careful not to use so much rice that it rubs off easily.

Dish Soap: A terrific wicked witch in New Jersey turned me on to this particular form of scrying, which can be done two different ways. The first is to take some pearly white dish soap and put it in a small glass jar with a little glitter and water mixed in. Light a candle and keep it nearby. Take the jar in hand and swirl it gently clockwise while thinking of your question. When you open your eyes, move the jar toward the candle so the glitter picks up the light. Now watch for specific movements in the soap or glitter, or for images to appear.

Here's a list of potential interpretations for the soap's movement:

Upward and to the right: A positive answer.

Downward and to the left: A negative answer.

Continuing in a circle without images: No answer available, things are too mixed up right now.

Bubbly in excess: Wishes are coming to the forefront.

Globs of glitter: Too much focus on the superficial; come back down to earth.

No glitter visible: Banish despondency and regain hope.

Swirling counterclockwise: Start thinking differently; you're looking at things the wrong way.

The alternative way to use dish soap is just to add it to your sink water. As you clean your dishes, keep your question in mind and watch the bubbles or soap residue as they move on the water. If images appear, make a mental note of them and look up interpretations later. I have a fondness for this particular method because it makes a chore I *hate* much more interesting.

Wax Drippings: All you need for this method is some candle ends and pieces and a bowl of cold water. I do recommend choosing the color of your candle so it somehow represents the question at hand (like red for matters of the heart or black when trying to uncover a potential hex). When all else fails, a plain white candle will do (even a birthday candle).

Sit down in front of the bowl and hold the candle in hand while you think of a question. Let the wax drip into the water for two to three minutes and make a pattern, then scry the pattern. Alternatively, let the wax drip onto a paper surface and then interpret the resulting image like you might an inkblot. The advantage to this second approach is that you can then carry the paper as a charm or amulet (like the rice) that provides continued perspective for the question you posed until the situation resolves itself.

Pendulums

Under normal circumstances, pendulums are considered fairly binary in nature (in other words, they're mostly used for yes-or-no questions). In order to increase the number of interpretive values that pendulums produce, you need to create a reading circle with drawings, objects or colors that represent a variety of answers. I generally recommend two sets of six symbols that are placed in mirroring locations on the left and the right of the pendulum circle, the left being a negative correspondence for that symbol and the right being positive.

Once the circle is assembled, your elbow goes outside it so that your arm is angled inward. The point of the pendulum (whatever form you've chosen) goes directly in the center. Still the movement with your free hand, close your eyes and think of your question. At some point you'll feel the pendulum moving. Observe its movements.

As already mentioned, movements on the right side (from twelve to six o'clock) are considered a positive aspect of that symbol, everything after six to midnight negative. To know which is which, see which part of the pendulum's swing is stronger. If it's pulling more powerfully to the right, that's positive; left, negative. The greater the range of movement, the more negative or positive the response.

If you can't set up a pendulum circle (or prefer not to), you can get the information desired here by asking a series of simple questions, stopping the pendulum between each query. Here's a list of movements and interpretive values as provided by traditional sources to help you prepare your questions and discern the resulting reading:

Clockwise movement: This indicates a yes, or positive response.

Counterclockwise movement: This is a no, or negative response.

Hesitation: There is uncertainty; proceed with caution.

> **Bobbing:** Two equally appealing options that have similar outcomes are present.
>
> **Up-down movement:** There is some type of divide or ego present.
>
> **Left-right movement:** Physical matters are at hand.
>
> **Ellipse (E-W):** Emotions play a key role here.
>
> **Ellipse (N-S):** There is a need for grounding.
>
> **Ellipse (diagonal):** Ethical considerations need pondering.

Herb/Plant Pendulum: To make this pendulum, all you need is a length of natural fiber string (slightly longer than the measurement from your pointer finger to elbow) and a leaf, petal or other easily secured plant part.

I recommend choosing the herb, flower or plant according to its metaphysical symbolism so that the overall energies harmonize with your question. For example, if you're asking about love, you might choose a rosebud or petals for the pendulum. If you were asking about fidelity or the success of an endeavor, you might choose a bay leaf. Refer to a good book on plant symbolism (like my book *The Herbal Arts*) to help in making this decision.

Next, fasten the herb to the string securely. Try to make sure the plant is evenly distributed in the knot. As you tie the knot, consider adding an incantation that also reflects your question. Returning to the two previous illustrations for love and success, the respective invocations might take this form:

> Love: *Rose of love, with magic round,*
> *Tell me do, is my love true?*
> Success: *Bay of power, bay of might,*
> *Is my victory within sight?*

You can continue repeating the incantation throughout the reading to support your efforts further.

Key Pendulum: I like using antique keys for this effort. There's something about the character of older items that appeals to me. Even so, any key with a hole at the top will work for this type of pendulum. Due to the powerful symbolism invoked by this object, key pendulums are especially suited to questions where you need to unlock a mystery of some sort, find the "key note" to a situation or discern the best opening available to you.

If you opt for the antique key, I recommend cleansing it in a bath of salt or lemon water before using it so it's free of residual energies. Also, consider dabbing the key with a sympathetic oil, or choosing the color of your string so it matches the question's theme. For example, if trying to figure out what's really bothering your significant other, you might dab the key with orange oil and use a pink or red string (both these items vibrate with love as a foundation for the inquiry). To choose between two appealing options, you might dab the key with ginger oil (success) and use a green thread to symbolize the "go-ahead."

As before, you can add an incantation and other sensual cues to this process to help. For example, I enjoy having music playing and a candle burning for almost every divinatory process I undertake. Something about the ambience puts me in the right frame of mind. You'll probably find similar devices or methods help you too.

Ring Pendulum: Rings have a lot of symbolic value in wicked witchery. They represent love, the sun and authority (gold rings), the moon (silver rings) and magic (when worn on the index finger). Rings were also among the favored forms for charms and amulets. With this in mind, you can choose a ring for pendulum work based on its symbolic value to you. A wedding ring obviously represents relationship questions, whereas a silver band with a crescent moon on it might symbolize questions surrounding the beginning of a project or personal cycle.

In either case, it's very important that you suspend the ring with the heavy side down (if there's a gemstone in the ring, this becomes the pendulum's pointer). Tying the ring in this manner helps assure the randomness of movement. And don't forget to get creative here. Consider adding several magical dimensions to this medium like those given in this chapter: Use color symbolism for the string, recite a knot spell while securing the ring, whisper an invocation, chant, burn incense, say a prayer or whatever. True wicked witchery responds to the moment with meaningful symbols, movements and thoughts. The more you do this, the more accurate your divination efforts become.

Practice Makes Perfect

Once you find or make a divinatory tool, start practicing with it. This is like a courtship period where you and your tool "get to know" each other! More important, practice time saturates the chosen medium with personal energy and familiarizes you with the symbolism so you don't always have to refer to an interpretive guide.

Do daily readings for yourself, and offer to do some for friends. Keep notes of your successes and failures so you can begin to recognize the time and conditions under which the best readings occur. I suspect you'll also notice that the accuracy of readings improves the more you work with your chosen medium.

While you're going through the courtship period, it's a good idea to start looking for a special housing for your tool. Be it a box, a pouch or a simple cloth wrapping, this cover protects the tool from random handling and others' energies. Along the same lines, periodically cleanse your chosen medium so residual vibrations don't hinder your efforts. This can most easily be accomplished by moving the tool through the smoke produced by sage incense (you can soak crystals briefly in salt or lemon water, wooden runes might be polished with lemon oil, et cetera).

At the end of the courtship period (I suggest three months minimum), you'll know if you're really happy with the chosen system. If you're not, this is the time to tweak it in the true spirit of wicked witchery. Make it right for you or don't use it! There's nothing that says you can't switch mediums if you made a bad initial choice.

By the way, as your proficiency in wicked witchery grows, the divination medium you've been using may start lacking the dimension desired. This is quite natural; a wicked witch's tools have to grow with him or her. At this juncture, it's time to either refine and expand the method you've been using or find one that suits the new person you're becoming. This is actually very exciting because it makes you intimately aware of personal progress, and gives you the opportunity to rethink your visionary tools using that progress as a guidepost.

Don't Overdo It

Even with all the benefits divination affords the wicked witch, it's not something you should overuse. If you can figure things out on your own, do so! Use divination only when you really need additional insight or perspective; depend on your own wisdom and judgment more so than on any tool or reading. See, witches are self-reliant sorts who like the sense of satisfaction that goes with our freedom to think, to choose, to act and to *be*. Our goal eventually is to become one with our magic so that tools aren't necessary. In the meantime, however, tools make our witchery a little easier, and often a little more fun!

⇒ four ⇐

Curses, Foiled Again

Curses are like young chickens,
and still come home to roost.
—Arab proverb

Dinna curse him, sir. I have heard it said
that a curse was like a stone flung up to
the heavens, and most likely to return
on the head of him that sent it.
—Walter Scott

What would any witch be without a handy set of spells and curses for all occasions? Nearly all ancient and modern magical books include a smattering of spellcraft. It seems that spells are a favorite, if not the most popular method of all time in the witch's kit.

There's a very good reason for this popularity. Casting a spell gives us something constructive to do when normal approaches have failed or stagnated. Rather than sitting and feeling helpless, we can grab our handy tools and start getting witchy. This, in turn, gets us thinking in a magical way—a way that opens us up to options that we hadn't considered before.

Reciting the words, mixing the components and going through the motions of a spell gives us a very real psychological edge, not to mention a magical one. Why? Because by definition spells work outside of ordinary means and processes to touch on the miraculous, just when we need it most!

Spells and Curses in History

Spellcraft's past is amazingly rich and diverse, having reared its head in every cultural setting and historical period. The Egyptians, for example, used poppets and the written word in spellcraft, regarding language as a powerful, divine gift. Later, the Greeks and Romans were known to use imitative spells a lot, illustrating to the powers exactly what they wanted to have happen (like pouring out water as part of a rain spell).

This doesn't mean the Egyptian methods disappeared. In fact, talkative merchants and traders dispersed magical techniques and tales along with the news of the day. As this information spread, it mingled with whatever magical knowledge existed in that culture, propagating the art.

The Arab trade routes in particular were filled to over-flowing with magical lore. The Arab caravan leaders knew that people valued magic, so they learned the folklore of spices and other goods and then cleverly used it to improve the value of their wares! A goodly portion of these beliefs came from their own heritage, including the few secrets imparted by local wizards who used herbs for spellcraft, often laced with complex incantations and sometimes the addition of knots to symbolically bind the energy in place. Much to their credit, we still find spells in modern collections that begin with knotting string, yarn or rope while reciting incantations.

In Gaelic regions, the word "spell" is *geis*, meaning "to entreat." This indicates the use of willpower and forceful words for spell casting. Malaysian sorcerers were trusted to banish ghosts or spirits whose presence negatively affected whole communities. They often donned costumes to help them commune with these powers. Meanwhile, on the other side of the world, Native American shamans were similarly putting on masks or body paint as part of spells to heal people, aid in vision quests, improve crop growth, bring rain or sun and generally attend to all the tribe's needs.

In Celtic beliefs, bards had the power of casting spells through their music and theatrics, neatly capturing the attention of the crowd (and likely a fair amount of coin too). In similar fashion, Druids (earth witches) throughout the British isle were known and feared for their spell-casting abilities. Some accounts speak of these tree-loving magicians standing on one leg with an eye shut and pointing a finger to make sure the energy went where it was intended. The bard's and sorcerer's purpose in using such elaborate methods were likely as much psychological as magical. After all, such a dramatic display makes a far more impressive impact than someone just looking at you intently!

Some common themes for spells in these and other traditions around the world include:

- finding love
- keeping mates from straying
- inspiring passion
- safeguarding one's possessions from theft
- overcoming an enemy or difficult situation
- resolving arguments or disputes
- protecting a home or person from ghosts, fairies, witches, demons and other undesirable spiritual forces
- recovering stolen or lost items
- making the land and crops fertile
- helping with conception and the delivery of children
- awakening one's psychic abilities
- cultivating wealth
- banishing sickness or augmenting health and longevity
- stimulating luck

So, we find that today's wicked witch isn't much different from his or her ancestors in terms of needs and goals. The main discernable difference is the way we design our spells (words, components, et cetera), but we're still using historical patterns as our guides. For example, the preceding given review of the world's spellcraft reveals several motifs that we can respectfully "borrow," including the use of knots, herbs, figurines, costume, written language, rhyme or music, incantations, willpower (as a driving force) and imitation as part of our art.

Additionally, it seems the wizards and witches in the ancient world weren't afraid of hamming it up, and modern witches today shouldn't be either! There's a special power in drama. Ever notice how people set aside logic when watching a movie, and just get caught up in the moment? Theatrical displays help shift the focus of both the magician and the observer away from temporal matters and toward spiritual ones. When circumstances allow, give it a try! Whip out your wand; let your voice grow strong until the air around you resonates with magical vibrations. Dance and sing your magic (if it helps, hop on one foot!). Do whatever it takes to build your energy into an intense cone of power. I think you'll find it liberating.

For Boon or Bane?

Spellcraft is definitely a two-edged sword. We can use our magic to bless or curse equally well. A curse is a type of wishcraft in which we willfully turn energy against someone as a hex. The reasons for this vary: revenge, anger, condemnation and personal gain, just to name a few. Ancient magical books are filled with these kinds of spells, most of which recommend ingredients that make even the wickedest of witches blanch a bit. And knowing the three-fold law, the modern wicked witch has to ask himself or herself: How much is a curse worth?

This isn't an easy question. Manipulation and evil intent are both considered "black" in nature—even more black than the clouds hovering around a pissed-off wicked witch on a really bad day! That doesn't mean that every white witch abstains from curses. He or she may periodically choose to accept the karmic kickback that goes with pushing the spiritual envelope into "gray" areas. Just bear in mind that this is always a *choice*. Whatever negativity you send out will find its way back to bite you on the butt, so it better be worth it!

Some people reading this will inevitably decide they want to dabble in gray areas. Consequently, I'd like to provide some precautions that will lessen the impact of the karmic boomerang. While I do not condone curses and other forms of negative magic, I know that it's something nearly everyone is likely to try at least once (myself included). Therefore, it's prudent to be wholly educated in how to handle these attempts as wisely as possible.

Step One: *Chill out!* Above all else, let yourself cool off before doing anything. For one, you might just change your mind during this time and opt for a better approach. For another, magic does not flow operatively when you're stressed and furious.

Hastily made magic born out of anger, pain and other negative emotions often makes for sloppy results. Why? Because you're not focused or centered. Rather than getting a finely tuned arrow of energy that hits its mark, you get an uncontrolled blast of static that generates metaphysical shrapnel. These nasty energy fragments can, and do, strike anything and anyone in their path, innocent or guilty, which changes the entire karmic equation dramatically.

Step Two: *Look for alternatives.* While you're calming down, seriously consider if there is another way to accomplish your goal without direct interference and magical manipulation. In the heat of the moment, it's easy to overlook sound, witchy options that are right in front of us. For example, say you get fired from a job. You could turn your magic against your employer, *or* you could use that energy to find a better job (returning to Rule Nine: Living well is the best revenge). The second option has no negative karmic impact.

Step Three: *Be sure you know your enemy.* Always get your facts straight before you act, and *never* cast a curse based on rumors, half truths or incomplete information. Doing so becomes a karmic double-whammy because you could easily direct your magical wrath at an innocent person. If you're not absolutely certain of the facts, and you still want to do something, please add some type of wording to your incantation that will negate the energy if it's misdirected (Rule Fifteen: Keep everything in balance and have fun).

Some witches rely on the universal clause "for the greatest good and it harm none," but this phrasing seems to defeat the purpose of a curse. You'll have to come up with your own way of handling this glitch in a manner suited to the situation and your personal path. A prayer for intervention by a god or goddess is one option here, allowing a greater wisdom to intercede and guide energy on your behalf.

Step Four: *Rethink your position and tactics.* Okay, you're calm now and sure of the facts. Ask yourself one more time if the curse is worth visiting yourself with similar energy thrice. If the answer is yes, go to the next step. If the answer is no, look at the spells in the rest of this chapter and find some witchy ideas that you can apply in a positive way.

Step Five: *Pattern your magical response.* In designing magical retribution, try to follow the exact pattern of what the person/group did to you, adding nothing extra. Mindfully return the negativity back to its source, blow for blow. This returns like for like, and isn't as malicious as other types of curses (per Rule Thirteen: Don't turn people into toads). Be aware, however, that the temporary exhilaration from getting even can quickly abate, being replaced by remorse or worry over what will soon be headed back your way.

Spellcraft Fundamentals

On a more positive note, there's nothing that says a wicked witch can't get really clever with his or her spellcraft in order to make life's difficult moments easier to bear. Before you can do that, however, you need to have a good grasp of how to create or adapt spells, and then how to use them effectively. This abbreviated overview acts as a kind of Spellcraft 101 to get you started.

Creating and Adapting Spells

Not every spell you come across will be right for your needs or your vision. Sometimes the wording seems awkward. In other cases, the components aren't available to you, or don't seem to make sense. In other instances still, the directions given in the spell are confusing or ill suited to our modern world. When these situations arise, we're left with one of two choices: Adapt the spell or start from scratch.

In my travels I meet a lot of people who are hesitant to tinker with existing spells or to make their own. But where would we be today if it weren't for experimentation? Old-fashioned trial and error has a long-standing role in magic—it's not as if a great tome of spellcraft just fell into someone's lap thousands of years ago. Necessity as the mother of invention helped to make personally attuned spellcraft a birthright, and one that a wicked witch revels in.

Here are some simple guidelines to get you started:

Ten Steps for Effective Spellcraft

1. Consider your goal in detail. What symbols, smells, sounds, et cetera represent that goal? The nature of spellcraft is such that the results will falter if you don't understand exactly what you want, why you want it and exactly what magical tools and emblems best symbolize both.

2. Look over existing spells that focus on this goal.

3. Determine if any of the existing spells can be used as they stand or adapted as a construct. If the spell needs to be adapted, ask yourself how. Remember that the process of adaptation is also part of the wicked witch's art—this is how you will make something new, something wholly yours, and leave your magical mark.

4. Gather the suggested components or the personally meaningful substitutes that you came up with in Step One and Step Three. Make sure any substitutes maintain the congruity of the spell and its purpose.

    By the way, some spells need nothing other than you as a component, notably those for charm, fascination or those involving the evil eye, which will be covered later in this chapter.

5. Design or adapt the spell's words and movements so they (a) feel right, and (b) work together to emphasize the desired energy. In so doing, keep your incantations short enough and the staging simple enough so you can memorize them. This

improves overall focus. For those who have trouble remembering incantations, try to make them rhyme. Rhyme is a good memory device with a distinct rhythm that adds a little extra energy into the equation. It doesn't have to be great poetry to work either.

6. Bear in mind that the most effective spells are those that include sensual cues (sounds, images, smells, tastes and textures) that match your goal. The more senses you can bring to your spellcraft, the more reliable the results will be. Return to insights from Step One to help you figure out how to add various sensual dimensions.

7. If possible, add propitious timing into the equation, like a waxing moon for positive, growth-oriented energy, or a waning moon for banishing and diminishing.

8. Determine if you want to cast the spell from within the safe confines of a sacred space. This isn't a requirement with spells focused on normal, everyday needs, but it is helpful. Sacred space keeps out unwanted influences and keeps your energy neatly in place until you're ready for Step Nine.

9. Fashion the spell so that it builds energy through the words and actions gradually, until it reaches a pinnacle. Remember to include a step that gives you a way of releasing the energy once it reaches that pinnacle, and guiding it toward its mark. Pointing a wand in the direction you wish your

energy to travel while reciting the final verse of an incantation is one example of this.

10. Finally, find a way to complete the spell's cycle. You opened the energy flow somehow, then released that energy. At the end of the spell working you need to close that flow (sitting down is one way).

You'll find that some of these steps appear in a slightly different form in the next section. That's because the way you create your spell and the way you cast it are intimately connected to the success of the working.

Casting Spells Effectively

Once you have all the details and necessary items for your spell in place, the next logical step is directing and releasing it. The first part is shaping our thoughts so that our will is keenly focused on the goal. Magic begins in your mind and heart. If things aren't clear here, the results won't be clear either.

The second part is projecting the magic outward from yourself toward the goal. I often describe this to people as an astral arrow. Your mind is the bow string that draws the arrow tight and helps you locate the goal. When you have the target keenly sighted with inner vision, you release the magical arrow. This doesn't mean you stop watching at this point! Keep visualizing that arrow heading where it needs to go until it passes the horizon. At this point, we must trust that we've done our work to the best of our ability.

Beyond shaping and projecting our will, here are some other hints that will make your spell casting, and indeed any magical method, more successful:

- **Self-preparation:** Make sure you're physically rested, spiritually attuned and mentally aware (Rule Four: Attitude is everything). Some witches like to take a shower or bath to purify their auras before working magic. If you're feeling really creative, add sympathetic herbs to the bathwater so that the vibrations fill your aura and support the magic. Here's a brief list of some of my favorite magickal bath aromas:
  - cinnamon for zeal (use sticks so you don't have to worry about clogging your drain)
  - cedar pieces for banishing negativity
  - lemon rind for cleansing and purification
  - marigold or rose petals for psychic awareness
  - lavender for peace
  - celery leaf or rosemary for mental focus
- **Tool/component preparation:** The objects that you use in *any* magical process should be properly cleansed so that no residual energies hinder or twist your magic (Rule Six: Practice sound spiritual hygiene).
- **Environmental preparation:** This phase includes setting up your tools and components so they're accessible, ensuring yourself of privacy (interruptions can derail your magic),

adding sensual cues and/or creating sacred space (which, in turn, purifies the space and makes it vibrationally ready for magic). To set up a magick circle see Augmenting Processes in Chapter 2.

- **Intuition:** Listen to your inner voice and that of Spirit. Just because you've planned a spell a certain way doesn't mean you can't change it if inspiration dictates (wicked witches are always flexible and adaptable).

- **Contemplation:** If circumstances don't allow for stating your incantation, chants or prayer out loud, think it purposefully instead. Thoughts have very real power. Remember: Witchery begins in the mind and will, and in some spells, those are the only components you'll be using.

- **Sanction:** Consider asking for the aid of a god or goddess who can guide your magic beyond the point where you can still see and sense its effects. This is especially wise if you're working in gray areas and don't want to risk visiting your negative energy on any- one or anything except the intended target.

- **Emulation:** Follow up the spell with tangible actions. I have generally found that Spirit answers honest efforts with positive out- comes, and each effort on your part gives the universe several opportunities to respond to your magical energy.

- **Repetition:** Repeat your spell as often as desired to support the magic and continue directing it effectively.

As you practice wicked witchery, you'll likely find other things that seem to improve your results. As you do, make a note of these so you can use them again and share them with other like-minded folk.

A Wicked Witch's Book of Shadows

A book of shadows is a collection of magic that reflects a specific metaphysical tradition or one created by a solitary practitioner. It's called a book of shadows for several reasons. For one, there have been occasions in history when witches had to meet in secret, in shadowy places, so that they wouldn't be persecuted or even killed for their beliefs. Second, by definition, magic works outside time and space, in the astral realm of potential and possibilities. Just as a shadow is an in-between place, our magic travels in between realities, just beyond ordinary perception.

The wicked witch's spellbook will, by its nature, be a little different than most modern collections. Yes, the traditional spells for health, wealth and happiness will appear there, but so will a lot of other things more suited to a wicked witch's resourceful nature. The following is just a sampling of such spells that you can copy into your own book of shadows, or adapt as you see fit. To increase the number of potential applications for these spells, just think in terms of opposites. For example, "drawing love" can become "turning away unwanted attention" by altering the timing of the spell, reversing the actions or changing the wording and components.

The Eyes Have It

Witches have long been feared for the power in their eyes, perhaps because of the old saying that goes, "Eyes are the windows of the soul." With time and practice a witch can learn to compel love and desire and can even curse with but a purposeful glance.

In this category of spells, we find two in particular that were very popular. First is the evil eye. At one time superstitions claimed that only those who inherited it, elderly witches or those with two differently colored eyes were thought to have this power, but pragmatics changed all that. When neither type of person was handy to blame for misfortune, another (often a woman) would be found and accused. And distance didn't matter. The evil eye could travel across distances as fast as a thought.

Interestingly enough, the spells I came across talk about turning away the energy of an evil eye, not how to cast it! They recommend carrying roan, juniper and iron bound in a red cloth and empowered with an incantation. This is still a perfectly good model to use. For the verbal component, try:

> *Juniper, iron and roan within,*
> *By my will the magic begins.*
> *Wrapped by cloth, bound and red-dyed,*
> *To protect me from the evil eye.*

But what about casting the evil eye, and can this be used in any manner other than cursing? The only "instruction" I could find, if you can call it that, was to stare intently while thinking and/or visualizing your desire. With such loose instructions, I see no reason why witches can't stare down anger, ogle for increased interest, gaze to take in some good vibrations or look up love!

This brings us to the second eye-centered spell: fascination. In reading about the art of fascination, it seems to be a kind of hypnotism in which energy is directed out of the eyes of the beholder into those of another person, specifically for love, passion or outright lust. Casting the fascination spell is pretty much the same as casting the evil eye (with different focus and intention, obviously). Look wanton! Think warm, sensual, wicked thoughts. Gaze in the direction of the person you desire (make sure you make eye contact), then let your body and eye language speak volumes!

To protect yourself from fascination (also sometimes called "charm"), one simple remedy says to steep a piece of coral in warm milk briefly, remove the stone and drink the milk or anoint yourself with it. To update this spell a bit, stir the milk counterclockwise and prepare it during a waning moon (both for banishing), while adding an incantation like:

> *Look away, look away.*
> *I need not your attention,*
> *My heart's here to stay.*

Family Feud

When people in your family have been bickering a lot, try this spell. Pick out one small item to represent each individual in your home (one that you don't mind disposing of). Take these outside and put them on the ground, saying:

I destroy anger, willfully treading it into the earth.

Step on the objects firmly, allowing your own anger to drain into them. Take these remnants and put them under a rock, saying:

Under this heavy stone I place our anger,
Never to return to it.
It is dead and buried away from me.
I release it. So mote it be.

If you're uncomfortable with the last bit of phrasing, both "amen" or "so be it" are perfectly good substitutions. Turn away from the stone and go home. Do *not* look back. So doing symbolically accepts back the negative energy buried there.

If, for some reason, you want to stir up an argument (sometimes simmering situations need to come to a boil to really clear the air), you can use the following spell instead. Begin by making a mixture of vervain, grain and corn. Vervain (an herb) has a purgative quality that was known even in ancient Rome, and corn/grain represents something positive growing where ill will dwells.

As you mix these two things, say:

Vervain and grain, release the pain;
Vervain and corn, let peace be reborn.

Put this in a location between yourself and the person that you want to confront (try using a potpourri dish, a vase or something similar that's unobtrusive). Finally, bring up the subject that needs to be tackled, and let the magic start working.

Good Fortune

In Teutonic tradition, one who wishes to win the favor of important people and improve their luck goes out and invokes the moon for aid. To try this, stand beneath a new moon, and say:

As the moon increases, so too my luck.

If you'd like to make a portable charm at the same time that will support your spell, hold a silver dollar beneath the moonlight and recite this incantation or something similar:

As the moon shines bright, so too my fate,
This coin with luck now saturate!

Carry the coin with you into any situation where you need a little extra luck or endorsement/support from an authority figure.

Impotency

Ancient spells that dealt with this problem were designed to cause or cure infertility or feebleness. However, there may be a larger application we can consider. The word "impotent" has two parts: im-potent, or lacking power! So you can use these spells to deal with physical issues, and also to confer, support, decrease or nullify a person's or situation's power!

Albertus Magnus, a great wizard of the 1500s, recommended a man pee through his wedding ring, and a woman spit into her breasts to restore passion and physical performance. *Voudon* tradition recommends making a wax figurine that accents the positive, reciting incantations over it and then keeping it near your bed! Conversely, to slow or halt passion or physical performance, magicians in the Middle Ages would tie knots and put them under the stairs or threshold of the person they wished to influence.

Adapting these methods is possible, but I suspect readers won't opt for Magnus's prescription. Many people shy away from being quite this "hands on" with witchery. But the idea of making a poppet holds a lot of potential and offers tremendous flexibility. You can fill the poppet with flowers or spices that represent your physical, mental or emotional goal, then charge it with an incantation.

For example, if your difficulty is physical, then you might take a poppet sewn from an old set of pajamas and filled with beans, cinnamon, mint and/or rosemary. All these items are magically aligned with maintaining potency and passion. As you sew up the final seam, say something like:

> *Herbs sewn in this doll so tight,*
> *Release without your magic might!*
> *Bring to me your staying power,*
> *Day to day, hour by hour.*

Visualize your goal while you work, then put this underneath your bed.

Or, to cool off a lover who's going too fast for your taste, make a poppet similarly, only fill it with little bits of cloth that have been knotted and some lavender for peacefulness. As you tie those knots say something like:

> *Your body must wait;*
> *Passion abate!*

Keep this in a sexually neutral room (like the living room), so it can infuse the air with calming energy.

Karmic Retribution

Have you ever wished that karma would catch up with someone *now* so at least you have the satisfaction of watching? This spell can help achieve that goal without manipulation.

Take the name of the individual in question written on paper (or a picture of them, or even an object that represents them). Wrap this image in reflective wrapping paper shiny side inward (silver or gold foil both work well) along with some sunflower seeds (these represent truthfulness). Tie this with a white thread so the bundle is secure, saying:

Away from me, your negativity;
Whatever you send out returns,
In your mind the truth burns!

Keep this bundle in a spot where it won't be disturbed. If you feel the difficulty might come up again, for example, put it in the freezer to halt action against you.

Legal Battles

Folk tradition instructs us to write our wishes on a large sage leaf and put it in our shoe before going into court. An alternative to sage is bay (sage promotes wisdom and magical manifestation while bay wards off negativity and promotes success). To improve the results add an incantation like:

The law is ever on my side,
While in my shoe this leaf abides.

After the hearing, burn the leaf as an offering (fire releases energy, and smoke continues promoting the spell).

Head 'Em Off

There are a lot of old spells that tell us how to stop an enemy, usually by rather drastic means. I'd like to offer these two spells as gentle but effective alternatives.

For the first, you'll need to know the person fairly well, and where they walk regularly. Once you find a soft imprint of their shoe in the ground, take a pin or nail and drive it into the soil, saying:

Slow down, slow down,
By my will you're bound.
You shall not make gains,
If ye be my bane!

The wording here is a little old, but it's important. This way, if you have a case of mistaken identity, that person will be completely free to continue their life unhindered by the spell.

A second example begins with an image of the person (a photo is best, but any symbolic item will do). Take this to a spot in the opposite direction of the area in which you don't want this person's influence felt. If possible, wait until a waning moon to improve the effect. Bury this in the soil, saying:

North, south, east, and west,
Pray attend to my behest!
I hereby conjure and constrain,
Your influence shall wane!

Heartbreak Hotel

When your heart is broken, magic can be a great healer. You can direct your spell to yourself to hasten the recuperative process, or you can direct a spell to the one who hurt you in an attempt to balance the scales. I prefer the former, but I'll provide examples of both here.

To return your sadness to the one who shunned you, take a pillar candle and carve the name of the person in it. This is best done at midnight with a pin or needle, saying:

> *You pierced my heart, and ripped it in twain.*
> *You shall therefore know my pain,*
> *From now until I'm whole again.*

Light the candle every day. During the time when it's ignited, that person will have no peace, up until you've healed emotionally (at which point the magic ceases).

Far more "white" in nature is this simple healing spell. Take a piece of red construction paper and cut out a heart. Tear this gently in two pieces. Now you'll need some sturdy tape and a healing salve (any commercial brand will do). Dab a bit of salve on each half of the torn heart, saying:

> *Pain shall cease; negativity release.*
> *Let healing flow; let my heart become whole.*

Tape the heart together, then fold it gently so you can carry it as a charm to help the healing process along.

Luring Love

In creating spells that draw love into your life, bear in mind that love cannot be manipulated if it's to have any lasting meaning. Even the loneliest of wicked witches wants to know that a lover or lifemate has *chosen* to be with him or her, not been constrained by magic.

With that in mind, I've patterned this love spell after one known in Etruscan tradition. For it, you'll need a broom, rose petals, apple peel, basil, orange rind and thyme. Put the herbs together in a bowl, saying:

Love be sweet, love be kind,
In these herbs my magic bind.
Rose for romance, apple for health,
Basil for zest, orange for wealth,
So my love and I will be of one heart and mind,
I blend herein a sprig of thyme.
And when I give them to the winds,
By my will this spell begins.

Take the herbs outside with your broom. Turn clockwise and sprinkle the herbs equally around you in a circle, repeating your incantation again. Finally, take the broom and sweep the herbs out from yourself (sending the energy), saying:

As I broom, as I sweep,
A lover to find, a lover to keep.

A second love spell begins with one strand each of pink, red and white yarn or cord. Braid these together, focusing on your goal to find a mate. Each time the strands cross, say:

The magic bind, true love to find.

Wear this in your hair, on a belt or somewhere else whenever you go into social settings so the magic can attract the right people your way. Note that if you're simply looking for temporary pleasure, you can change the incantation to something like:

"The magic bind, passion to find."

Money Matters

The variety of spells meant to improve one's financial security are nearly overwhelming. I'm going to provide a couple of options here as patterns for your adaptation, but please know that the world's folk traditions offer many more options for your consideration.

- Plant a silver coin somewhere near your doorway so that money "grows" and prosperity is attracted into your home (English custom).
- Find or make a bookmark that represents a god or goddess of abundance and keep this in your checkbook (adaptation of a spell from India).
- Carve into a green- or gold-colored candle dollar signs and anoint it with patchouli oil (associated with financial security). Light this, saying: "As this candle decreases, may my money increase." Let the candle burn completely out (common form of candle magic).

- Keep the cork from a bottle of champagne that you enjoyed on a celebratory occasion (especially one associated with a raise or windfall). Split the cork at the top and put a silver coin therein, saying: "Money to me, money to me, today I claim prosperity." Keep this in a special place of honor in your home (adaptation of a Scottish tradition).
- Mix hand cream with a few drops of any aromatic oil that represents prosperity (ginger and mint are two good choices). Rub this over your hands before balancing your checkbook or entering into any financial transactions, saying something like: "Keep my pockets filled, by my word and my will" (an adaptation of an old European folk spell for fortune).

Passion Plays

In Ceylon, it's traditional to speak incantations over a flower, then present it to the one you desire, to release the magic. Adapting this, you might get a passionflower (the symbolism is apt) or a red rose and empower it by saying:

Within burns a fire,
Let it light our desire!

Leave this in the room where you and your significant other will be making love.

Conversely, if you want to tone down the passion in a

relationship, boil a bit of cedarwood with bay leaves before your guest arrives. Sprinkle the resulting tincture around the area where you spend most of your time, saying:

Magic's around, slowing us down.
Hesitate, wait! Let passions abate!

Dab a bit of any remaining tincture on yourself to improve your sense of control.

Spell Turning

For this spell, you'll need some powdered myrrh and a fire source. During a waning moon sit before the fire source holding the myrrh in your strong hand. Visualize all the energy of the spell in question leaving you and pouring into the myrrh. Toss the myrrh into the fire, saying:

Turn the magic, away the evil eye!
The spell shall wane, by and by.
Burned in the fire, back to them who bewitched me,
I declare myself free of this sorcery!

Let the fire burn completely out, then gather some of the ashes to carry as a protective amulet.

Addendum

In reviewing the rich lore of witchcraft and magick, I found a couple of interesting tidbits that may help your spellcraft along when other approaches aren't working. First is working with hair, a place where a witch's power was said to reside. Modern practitioners still feel that adding a strand of your hair to any spell marks the magic with your personal energy signature, and letting down your hair during spell casting increases the power created. Similarly, using a strand of hair from someone else is an excellent way of directing magic toward them.

Second is whistling up your wishes and desires. Witches in Scotland and other parts of the world were often credited with being able to whistle up the wind. The ever dexterous wicked witch, however, uses this power for much more than casting weather spells. For example, we might whistle to the north, south, east or west as a way of directing magic and empowering it with the elemental energies of a specific wind (earth, fire, air and water, respectively). Or, as part of a spell for joy, we might whistle a "happy tune"!

The air element involved here bears the symbolism of movement, refreshment, shifting attitudes and relief. This means that whistling would be a suitable component in any magic aimed toward these (or related) goals. Just whistle up a motivating wind, a refreshing breeze, some fresh air for new perspectives and a cooling gust to quell anger!

There are certainly many more spells that you will eventually want to add to your wicked witch's book of shadows. You'll also want to include a few charms, rituals, potions and other magical tidbits that can round out your book with a variety of methods suited to a similar diversity of goals. With that in mind, let's move on and look at other favorite tools for wicked witches: charms, amulets, talismans and fetishes.

≩ five ≨

The Wicked Witch's Knapsack (Portable Magic)

*There are few sporting men who are not
in the habit of wearing charms and talismans.*
—Thorstein Veblen

Who says you can't take it with you (your magic, that is)? Expressing and emphasizing our witchy nature means finding ways to make magic an active part of our lives, no matter the circumstances. Our ancestors were wise to this idea and came up with a kind of spellcraft that answered this need. Specifically, they designed portable charms, amulets, talismans and fetishes for themselves and others. Whenever such an object was carried, its magical energy emanated from the bearer to promote health, attract love, inspire prosperity and answer other common needs.

How did an object manifest such power? Think of charms and amulets like empty batteries. You can charge these objects (stones, plant parts, coins, jewelry or whatever) with the magical power generated by a spell. This results in a mystically enhanced token that lets you carry a spell in your back pocket and release its associated energy slowly. This energy then fills your aura and environment with the right vibrations to help manifest your goal(s).

The Advantages of Magical Tokens

Periapt (token) creation offers many advantages to the wicked witch in terms of flexibility and creativity. In particular, you can:

1. Choose a personally meaningful token that has sympathetic value for your magic. Note that many of the ancient charms and amulets were made into jewelry (rings, pendants, lockets and the like) so this helps you fulfill Rule Five: Look good and always accessorize!

2. Design a portable token for long-term, short-term or even one-shot magical uses (fetishes in particular often fall into the last category).

3. Contrive the magic so it can be turned on and off as needed by giving the token a power phrase or by rubbing it while reciting your incantation again

(examples of this will be provided throughout this chapter).

4. Fashion easily carried objects that provide all the same energy signatures (love, health, peace, et cetera) for which spells can be designed. Better still, most of these objects are subtle in their magic and very nondescript if anyone should happen to see them (in other words, they don't scream "witch").

5. Make a bunch of these all at once (keeping several set aside for your car, the office or wherever you feel the need, but where you might not have the freedom of spellcraft).

6. Carry a variety of charms and amulets at the same time. This provides a mixture of energies according to your need. For example, one might carry a love charm and a peace amulet when overly stressed about a relationship.

7. Create great gifts for witchy friends and family that reflect that person's needs or goals, like prosperity, good luck or health.

Since amulets and charms (in the broadest sense) are directly related to spells, we find them among the oldest forms of witchery. And like so many other types of folk magic, most don't require a lot of time to make. Wicked witches today (even those with hectic schedules) should be able to add this technique into their repertoire with very little fuss.

Clarifying Terms

In an effort to follow Rule Eleven, Learn the lingo, I'd like to share with you a brief overview of what makes a charm a charm, versus an amulet, talisman or fetish. From the get-go you should know these objects are intimately intertwined in magical history. In some instances, it's very hard to separate one from another (especially since the terminology hasn't always been applied correctly). So, what I'm presenting here are the technicalities—what you see in other books may vary from this foundation.

Amulet: Amulets are protective in nature, often having been used to ward off the influence of witchcraft, evil or other harmful influences. In Greek tradition, amulets were called *amylon*, meaning "food." They got this title because people used small food offerings to appease and propitiate spirits.

Later, and in other parts of the world, people designed more durable amulets for carrying, keeping in the home or placing with valued possessions. Since the amulet bears preventive magic, its power remained neutral until called into action by a situation or until activated by the bearer. This continues to be true today.

Many ancient amulets were very expensive, having been made out of precious stones and metals and decorated with intricate carvings. Practitioners felt that the purer and more valuable the base materials, the more powerful the magic. This is one part of amulet creation that the budget-minded wicked witch avoids. On the other hand, if you have access to certified organics or better-than-average quality mediums for your amulets, they're worth considering.

Good examples of amulets that many people use today without even knowing it are a garlic braid hung in the home to ward off malevolent spirits and carrying a St. Christopher metal for safety.

Charms: Simply defined, a charm is any object that houses power designed for personal gain or to ward off a particular type of energy. This object is empowered by the singing or speaking of spells over it (charm comes from the Latin *carmen*, meaning "song"). Thankfully, any wicked witch that can cackle can certainly learn to intone a spell—it need not be operatic! Charms also take written form (on cloth or paper). In this case, having poor penmanship won't hurt anything; it will neatly conceal your magical intention!

Unlike amulets, which are passive until something external activates them (usually a specific vibration), charms exercise their influence all the time (this is part of the attraction for wicked witches. We like having magic flowing 24/7!). The most popular applications for charms historically were to draw luck, improve the outcome of a hunting expedition, secure love, inspire passion, protect the bearer from fairies or other mischievous spirits and return stolen property. They remain so to this day!

An enduring example of charms are the small objects (shoes, anchors, hearts, et cetera) designed for bracelets. These pieces of jewelry, aptly called "charm" bracelets, originally had magical meaning for those who wore them, or received them as gifts. Each charm provided specific energy, the heart representing love, the anchor symbolizing security and so forth.

Note that no matter the form your charms take, the effect of most is temporary. They're not meant to last for a long time. So, if you're going to keep such an object for years, it's best to recharge it regularly using the original spell. How often will depend much on your environment and how frequently the energy in that item is put to the test.

Fetish: Our Victorian ancestors sometimes used this word to describe the charms and amulets that came from Africa, which was somewhat incorrect. A fetish is any object thought to bear a beneficial spirit. It can also allude to an item that's been blessed by a higher power (invoked through a verbal incantation), or one that creates a strong emotional response (like statues or medals of saints). For the purposes of this book, we'll be focusing on the latter fetish, the former requiring a high degree of magical skill to create.

Fetishes were sometimes used in shape shifting and glamoury. In fact, some magical historians feel that Uther Pendragon used a fetish as part of his magical disguise to fool Ygraine into thinking he was her husband. I'm not exactly sure why this type of magic found a niche with fetishes, but I suspect it was because wizards trusted in (a) the power of the indwelling spirit, (b) the power of the deity invoked or (c) the power of emotion to create illusion.

Besides the application in illusionary magick, many witches like to make disposable fetishes, suited for one use. To activate this type of fetish and its power, it can be ritually thrown away (to banish something), the components scattered (to disperse a spell to several people or over an area), the bundle burned (to release the energy quickly) or the token buried (so the energy grows or grounds out).

Talisman: A talisman is an object bearing a power, a spirit or an energy signature whose positive effect is somehow conferred upon its owner. In humankind's past, a talisman wasn't just left lying around the magical workroom either, which is why it's an excellent addition to the wicked witch's knapsack. Talismans were adapted to many magical methods, like a witch's wand becoming a talisman for shape shifting, or Moses' rod becoming a talisman for elemental manifestation (water).

Like fetishes, some talismans were thought to have indwelling spirits whose power made the talisman work. Unfortunately, this becomes a problem if the spirit doesn't like the person wielding the tool! So, most wicked witches today opt to simply use special timing and incantations to empower a talisman rather than invoke a spirit. This means that the element of timing sets a talisman apart from charms (charms *can* benefit from auspicious astrological timing, but it's not a required part of the process of making them).

In addition to being created at a special time, the base material for a talisman must be suited to the task.

For example, one might charge an amethyst for clear-mindedness at noon in order to saturate the stone with talismanic virtue. Why? Because amethyst has long been revered for its ability to overcome intoxication (which would, in turn, clear one's mind), and noon is an hour that emphasizes our cognitive, reasoning abilities.

Applying the Art

The way we define these items isn't half so important as the way we apply them. Really, the processes are so similar to one another that the jargon here simply pleases perfectionists. So, don't sweat it. I promise that there won't be a quiz later!

To help you use the remainder of this chapter effectively, I've set it up by theme rather than by type of object. For example, Just Humor Me talks about making a token that keeps your sense of humor intact. This way you can find a subject that comes close to your need or goal, read over the options provided there and find something you can use or adapt.

Attractiveness: Since we want to heed Rule Five, Look good, magic for comeliness, allure and appeal are all part of the wicked witch's knapsack. There are many times in my life when I need a magical boost to the ego or minimally a self-assurance nudge, and I'm sure I'm not alone. Consequently, these fetishes are designed with beauty in mind!

To make any of these you'll first have to decide what aspect of the god/dess you want to call upon to empower and bless them. Some suggestions include Venus, Aphrodite, Apollo and Zeus, but there are plenty of others depending on your exact goal. In making this decision it's best if you have an understanding of the deity (preferably a working relationship with him or her), and know how to say his or her name correctly (how would you feel if someone asked you a favor preceded by mispronunciation?).

The first fetish is based in a hand mirror since so much of our self-perception is established with this device. In this case you might call upon a god/dess who is associated with mirrors, like Tezcatlipuco (Mexico), who presides over matters of perception! You'll also need heather oil (or a homemade tincture made from steeped heather flowers in warm water).

Hold the mirror in one hand and dab the heather oil on it with the other, moving clockwise while you invoke your chosen god/dess, saying:

> Hail _____! [fill in with the Being's name]
> Come to this mirror and fill it with your radiance!
> Come to this mirror, here let magic dance!
> Come with beauty and power that others might see
> The god/dess in all, the god/dess in me!

Whenever you feel your confidence waning, look in the mirror to see the god/dess shining there!

The second fetish uses dried rosemary and a small container in which to carry it. Take the bundle and invoke your chosen god/dess, saying:

> *Hail _____! [fill in with the Being's name]*
> *Saturate this herb with your enchantments,*
> *Saturate it with radiance!*
> *When in my shoes this herb is scattered,*
> *The magic release, my attributes flatter!*

Just as described in the incantation, put a pinch in your shoes when you want your best characteristics to shine to others. Better still, rosemary is a natural deodorizer, so you'll always have sweet feet!

Just Humor Me: This amulet is designed to help you follow Rule Eight, Keep your nails and your wit sharp, and Rule Fifteen, Have fun. One of the best components for a humor amulet is a feather (to "tickle your fancy"). Any feather will do, but you might want to get one in a color that you like (craft shops often carry a variety).

Wrap the feather in white cloth (for protection), saying:

> *When laughter seems lost, bring this to mind,*
> *Joy within this cloth I bind.*
> *Humor be quick, smiles be kind,*
> *Bring this magic ever to mind!*

Carry the token or keep it in a spot where you know your sense of humor will need some support.

An alternative method to bolster verbal humor begins with a carnelian. The Spanish praised this stone for its capacity to improve the bearer's communication skills, so you're simply going to be directing its energy more specifically. Hold the carnelian under a bright ray of sunlight (humor is a conscious ability that requires a quick mind) and recite an incantation, like this one, five times (five is the number of versatility and resourcefulness):

A silver tongue grant;
As this spell I incant.
My mind and words be quick to find,
Humor of the funniest kind!

You can then use this charm in a variety of ways. It can be carried into situations where you really need to be "on." It can be steeped in water, then you drink the water to internalize a dose of good humor for the day, or you can rub the stone to release a little of the magic within when the levity is needed. After you've used the stone five times, recharge it.

By the way, the concept of repeating an incantation a specific number of times to support specific goals is a very old and venerable custom among witches. If you'd like to consider using or adapting this technique yourself, here's an overview of numerical correspondences for your reference:

Numeric Correspondences

1 the sun, birth, beginnings, the self, harmony

2 duality, symmetry, attentiveness, truth, beauty

3 the goddess, luck, fate, virtue, justice, fortitude

4 the elements, wind magick, foundations, maturity

5 protection, safety, duty

6 love, fertility, self-control, productivity

7 completion, spiritual gifts, wisdom, diversity

8 time, rebirth, justice, transformation, authority

9 completion, creativity, mastery, adeptness

Loves Lost: Wicked witches make great lovers. But, despite all our powers, when love ends it's often very hard to break the ties and get on with our lives. This one-use fetish will help. Begin by taking any flammable item (that you don't mind burning) given you by your ex. Create a safe fire (preferably one made without chemicals in the protection of a sacred space). Toss the chosen item into the fire, speaking out loud your ex's name, followed by this incantation:

> *Burn, burn, let my love turn.*
> *This fire shall sever, our love forever.*

Carry the remaining ashes until your heart heals, or bury them far away from you in order to bury the past.

If you feel the relationship has a chance of being

rekindled, make this talisman during a waxing moon. Freeze the name of the one you love in an ice cube. Then let it melt beneath the moonlight, saying:

As the moon grows full,
Remember the fulfillment of our love.
As the ice dissipates,
May your anger abate.

Carry the remaining piece of paper with you into the next meeting you have with this person to encourage a reconciliation.

An alternative reconciliation fetish begins with a piece of dragon's blood (an herb) and a fire source. Hold the reddish powder in your hand, saying:

Your heart is free, your will is free,
But if it's meant to be, return to me!

Toss the herb in the fire and let it burn completely. Carry the ashes afterward until you know (one way or the other) what direction the relationship is going to take. If separation is imminent, release the ashes to the wind to freely release that person and your ties to him or her. If reconciliation occurs, give half the ashes to your beloved as a love charm.

Love Found: The same cautions apply to love-drawing tokens as to love spells: Don't try to orchestrate other people's feelings. That having been said, to encourage love in your life, try this simple verbal charm. Every night for an entire month, go out just as it gets dark and watch for the first star to appear. As it does, recite this incantation, focusing on the personality qualities you'd like in a companion:

> *Love, love, from my heart pours,*
> *Let love find its way to my door!*

Watch to see who shows up at your house or apartment (like people doing surveys, salespeople, et cetera). You might be surprised to discover one of them has all the right attributes you want in another person.

An alternative love charm begins with two pieces of red cloth, each cut in the shape of a heart. Stitch up all but the top of the heart and stuff the center with dried rose petals, saying:

> *Love to me, the magic is free!*

Then sew up the last side of the heart, saying:

> *The perfect mate within each stitch,*
> *By my will I release this wish!*

Carry the heart with you regularly to attract the right people into your life.

To inspire devotion in an existing relationship, sow a flowering plant somewhere that you can tend it regularly. As you secure the plant in the ground, say:

With each wind that blows, let love grow.
My heart to thee, turn yours to me!

Take a petal or leaf, placing it in your shoe as a portable charm that inspires fidelity (so love "walks with you"). Each time you return to care for the plant, recite the incantation again to strengthen the spell. If you notice the plant growing ill, stop using it for magickal purposes unless you want to have feelings also "die."

Lucky Charms: By far the most popular tokens in the wicked witch's complement, luck bears energies that can help just about any situation. Here are just a few charms for you to consider, but there are lots more, some components for which you probably already have somewhere. Like what? How about a coin you've kept since childhood, or a tumbled stone you found at the beach? Maybe that first dollar you ever earned, or the rose petals you saved from a congratulatory bouquet. All these things represent a kind of good fortune, so their matrix is perfectly suited to absorb the power of your luck spell!

The first good luck charm begins with any type of skin cream you like (an aloe-based cream is a good choice, if available, because it conditions the skin pleasantly even as you hope to create a smooth path for luck). To this, add a few drops of rose oil, then put a small amount in a portable container, saying:

Luck with people be born,
Whenever this cream is worn!

Note that you can change the word "luck" here to "favor" if it better suits your need. Dab the cream on your wrists or hands so the energy is exchanged with a handshake!

A second luck charm begins with marigold and chrysanthemum petals gathered at dawn (the time of renewed hope). Gently clean the petals of any residue and dry them. Keep these in an airtight container (add some essential oil if you wish for a pleasing aroma) and bless them, saying:

Petals of power, of serendipity,
Bring lots of good luck back to me!

Whenever you need a little extra luck, sprinkle a few out to the winds or carry them with you all day, then release them.

Finally, to bring more luck into your home, make a charm of mistletoe and sage bound together and leave it near your door. This is a natural charm that has all the right energies so that good fortune will find you.

Money Makers: Money can't buy happiness, but wicked witches aren't naive. We know that being financially secure frees up a lot of energy that can be used in magic. With that in mind, here's some pocket magic designed to improve your financial security. Pick a marigold every day at noon for a month and carry this with you in your pocket or purse (near your wallet). This is a natural charm for prosperity.

Alternatively, take any silver coin (real silver is better

than silver toned) and take it outside on the night of a new moon (just waxing). Turn this talisman in your pocket (to turn money your way), saying:

> Green and silver and gold,
> Money to keep, money to hold.
> Lady moon, my wishes see,
> Bring to me prosperity!

Carry the coin with you and rub it any time you're focusing on financial matters (like when you're considering an investment).

A third prosperity charm begins with a dollar bill. Dab a bit of patchouli or cinnamon oil on the corners of this bill, saying:

> No matter where this roams,
> Prosperity follows to my home.

Put the dollar bill in an envelope and address it to yourself. Mail it from a location other than your home (maybe the post office or your workplace), and let money follow it back to your doorstep. When the dollar gets back to you, carry it as a charm so that no matter where you go, prosperity will follow you back (just be sure not to spend it)!

Protective Pieces: You are not the only wicked witch in the world, and there are a lot of people or situations that don't have your best interest at heart. So returning to the wicked axiom of "forewarned is forearmed," the next few amulets are designed to safeguard what you have, and keep away those negatives that you don't need.

Health: This is a neat little talisman/fetish that begins with a pack of matches (note: if you can find incense matches, all the better—the aroma can correspond to your goal. There's a reference list in Chapter 1 for your use). Hold the package in your hand during a waning or dark moon, saying:

Flames that destroy, oh defending fires,
banish all that is unhealthy, harmful or dire,
Sickness of any kind, by my words and my will I bind.
Health captured within
When the fire's ignited, the magic begins!

Light a match and let it burn completely out any time you feel yourself getting ill. When you're out of matches, just make a new amulet!

An alternative pattern for a health amulet comes from a very ancient and still very practicable Gnostic spell. It begins with the word "abracadabra," which roughly translated from a Chaldean word means "to diminish." Thus, the term was written in a diminishing form, the full word at the top of a triangle and only the "a" at the bottom, to create a healing amulet that would cause the malady to shrink! Oddly, this amulet wasn't carried, it was usually nestled in a tree, likely to put sickness away from oneself.

To make an amulet like this one, suited to the wicked

witch's knapsack, just write a word that describes your problem in diminishing form on paper. For example, if you have migraines, the amulet would look like this:

migraine
migrain
migrai
migra
migr
mig
mi
m

Dab this paper with a health-promoting oil like lotus, sandalwood or rosemary (this doubles as aromatherapy). Then each night before you go to bed, put the amulet on your forehead (applying the magic where it's most needed). Carry the amulet to offset the chance of getting a migraine away from home.

Home: One of my favorite house amulets begins with four coins and four stones. The coins can be lucky pennies, coins from the year of your birth or with some other meaningful attribute (color, country of origin, et cetera). Choose the stones (if possible) for their elemental correspondences. For example, agate, jet and turquoise are earth stones. Amber, obsidian and quartz are fire stones. Aventurine, jasper and pumice are air stones and amethyst, coral and sodalite are water stones.

After gathering the necessary components, try to figure out where the four main compass points lie in your home. You'll want to find accessible spots near those points to store your stones and coins (so you can recharge the amulets regularly). As you place one coin and the appropriate stone in its designated spot (starting in the east and moving clockwise), say:

> A *lucky coin and the Power of winds,*
> Protect *my home as this spell begins.*
> (*moving to the south*)
> A *prosperous coin and the power of flame,*
> Protect *my home, all negativity tame.*
> (*moving to the west*)
> A *loving coin and the power of rain,*
> Protect *my home from all who wish bane.*
> (*moving to the north*)
> A *providence coin and the power of earth,*
> By *my will to this magic give birth!*

Repeat this process whenever you feel the protective energy needs reinforcement (you don't have to pull out the tokens, just dust them off, put your hands over them and recite the incantation again purposefully).

An alternative way of protecting your home is using an old-fashioned witch bottle buried nearby. No one is really sure where the idea for these came from, but it's certain that a clever wicked witch somewhere got the ball rolling! To make this jar you need to collect unsavory ingredients during a waning moon (anything sharp, stinky, sticky, gooey or just plain icky). Put these in a glass jar mixed together, and secure the top with rubber cement (so that if animals or children accidentally dig up the jar, they won't be harmed by the contents).

Wait until the dark moon to bury the jar. As you put it in the ground, say something like:

Gather evil into your briars;
Reflect negativity and malintent back to its sender.
All ill will or any blight,
Snatch from the air and bind it tight!

Cover the jar completely with soil and leave it. If you ever notice a lot of problematic things happening around your home rather suddenly, see if the jar has been disturbed or broken. If so, replace it.

On the Road: Our society is very mobile, and wicked witches seem to be always on the move. So, it's nice to have one or two protective amulets that we can take with us while we're running hither and yon.

Keeping this in mind, one of my favorite protective tokens is what I call a portable altar. It can be created in any size suited to your need. For example, if you want one for your car, it needs to be of a size that fits neatly in the glove compartment, or of a design suited to hanging from your rearview mirror. For yourself, you'll want something pocket-size or suited to a briefcase, purse or wallet. Mine takes the form of an old pillbox with a latch lid.

Once you find a container that has a sealing top, put the ashes from a ritual fire in it along with small tokens from the elemental world, like a tiny crystal (earth), a feather (air), a seashell or sand (water) and a match (fire). As you put each inside the container, say:

> By earth I'm grounded
> (put the crystal in),
> By air I'm cushioned
> (put the feather in),
> By water I'm buoyed
> (put the shell in),
> By fire I'm protected
> (put the match in).
> All within this little jar,
> To keep me safe from all harm.
> So be it!

Seal the top and put the container where you most need it.

Change the components of this spell to suit the size of your container. For example, if you have a very small container, you might use powdered herbs that have the right elemental correspondences for filling it (like ginger or cinnamon for fire, a pinch of oatmeal or a piece of unpopped popcorn for earth, sage or a grain of rice for air and thyme or a piece of orange rind for water). A good reference book in which you can find the elemental listing of hundreds of herbs is *Cunningham's Encyclopedia of Magical Herbs*.

Psychic Baubles: Wicked witches depend heavily on their ability to sense trouble before it's brewing, so having a couple of psychically enhancing tokens benefits us tremendously. It means we can rely a little on our pocket magic to guide us, rather than having to stop and extend our senses (something that takes time and effort).

If possible, psychic baubles might be best chosen from things that you wear on or near your head (since the psychic center is the third eye in the middle of your forehead). Earrings (especially for developing clairaudience, or clear hearing), a scarf, a hat, barrettes, hair clips and glasses (especially for psychic vision) are all good examples. Alternatively, if you simply want a charm to carry around, quartz crystals or amethysts are both good choices. They're durable and natural psychic amplifiers.

Consider dabbing your chosen object with a little sympathetic oil. The smell turns into magical aromatherapy and improves the strength of the token. Some good choices for scents include sandalwood and lilac.

Finally, put your hands palm down over the item, saying:

> Give to me hands that sense,
> Energies in truthfulness.
> Give to me the ears to hear,
> Spirit's whispers when it's near.
> Give to me the eyes to see,
> Magic without, and the magic in me!

If you wear or carry this item often, remember to recharge it at least every three months, or when you feel like your psychic senses aren't as keen as they should be.

Retaliation and Rivalry Trinkets: What wicked witch doesn't want to get even once in a while, or at least trip up a rival at a perfectly embarrassing moment? This is normal human nature, and a desire that our ancestors seemed to have had in abundance! The spells here are adapted from various ancient sources so they suit our world and magical ways today.

The first one is simply a verbal charm. Go somewhere that you can be insured of some privacy and where you can recite your incantation/chant out loud, as loudly as you wish. Visualize in great detail what happened in your life that brought you to this moment. As you feel yourself really focused on the ill deed, begin to repeat the following incantation, whispered at first:

Seek out the one who did this deed,
That it return to them thrice, by magic's creed!

Continue to repeat this phrase louder and louder until you can sense the energy has reached a pinnacle. Open your arms as if to release that cone of power, then trust in the charm to do its work. If something happens to make it seem like the perpetrator is up to his or her old tricks again, you can repeat this incantation mentally to revitalize the spell's original effect and energies.

A second amulet comes from the voodoo tradition and requires that you know for certain both the person who has harmed you, and where that person lives. To make this amulet, gather rusty nails and briars, wrap them in red flannel, bind them with a white string and say:

Capture _____ *'s negativity,*
From his/her ill will I shall be free!

Fill in the blank with the name of the person, then bury or hide the bundle on their property. This works like a remote witch bottle that confines that person's malevolence toward you.

The third talisman begins with one red and one white string or cord. Tie them together nine times, saying:

It is not this string I bind, but _____ *'s wicked ways.*
Separate them from me,
And keep his/her magic at bay!

Fill in the blank with the person's name, and make sure to repeat your incantation at the tying of each knot. Keep this device in a safe place until you feel the problems stemming from that individual have completely rectified themselves, then untie the knots and burn or bury the string so as to keep that whole situation in the past, where it belongs.

The fourth charm was adapted from Albertus Magnus's work, and is designed specifically to get an unwanted rival/guest to leave your company. For it, you'll need a candle carved with the initials of the individual in question. Go somewhere private (the bathroom is ideal) and light the candle. As it burns down to the initials, say:

He/she will forever fart,
Until they concede and from my presence depart.

You can imagine the resulting physical condition that would eventually lead to that person leaving (yet, it's not an overly harmful spell, more embarrassing than anything else!).

Last but not least, to bring enmity between your lover and a rival for his or her attentions, you'll need a piece of straw. This represents the "straw that broke the camel's back" and you can get a piece from your kitchen broom. Take the straw and recite the name of your lover and the rival over it, saying:

> *Your attraction is broken in twain,*
> *Any undo attentions disdain.*

Break or cut the straw very purposefully, burning one half and carrying the other half with you until that situation rectifies itself.

Success Sorcery: Most witches are very tenacious about success. To us this isn't just a word, it's a way of living. Success doesn't mean walking over people or getting somewhere if we don't deserve it. What it does mean is applying ourselves and our magic to the greatest capacity possible. These bits of portable magic help with that aim.

The first is called the key to success, which aptly has an old skeleton key for a component. Why a skeleton key? Because these often opened many different kinds of locks in their day; the symbolism here is that any door is open to us if we use magic as a key!

You can easily find these old keys at flea markets and garage sales. Bind a strand of your hair to any part of the key during a waxing moon (or on a Monday, which is the moon's day). After you tie the hair in place, add an incantation like,

Turn the tide so it flows my way,
(then turn the key clockwise in the air)
Bring success by night, achievement by day.

Attach this to your key chain! If your hair ever detaches or breaks off, you'll need to redo the spell to energize this talisman again.

The second charm is designed to induce success through the positive and determined use of personal skills. (Wicked witches aren't afraid of applying a little elbow grease to help magic's gears move more smoothly.) It begins with a bloodstone, which was one of the first stones used in magic, popularly carried by soldiers into battle for victory and by others for positive outcomes in legal matters.

Hold your stone first in your weak hand, saying:

Success fulfill, success be mine
(switch to your strong hand, the one you write with)
By this magic let my skills shine!

Carry the stone into situations that exercise your talents so that others notice your efforts more, and will give you the credit that's due.

Work Management: Most people have a job outside the home at least part of the week. Within those jobs we're often faced with difficulties that beg to be whipped into shape by the wicked witch's wand! While you might not be able to do this at the office, there's nothing that says you can't devise some pocket magic to take with you every day, depending on the need at hand.

In considering what types of magic I thought you might want in your workplace, I came up with three things that everyone talks about. The first is the ability to organize and focus on a job. To improve your time management skills, begin with a pen that has replaceable cartridges and a tiny square of paper upon which you've written the words "focus" and "detail" (or something similar). Roll this paper around the pen's cartridge so it's inside (you can adhere one end with a snippet of tape to make this easier). As you wrap, say:

My thoughts are keen, my eyes are sharp,
To my mind, focus impart!

Carry the pen in a pocket or purse, keep it at your desk, set it near your computer, put it in an organizer or someplace else that you can use it regularly, especially when you feel preoccupied.

The second type of job magic is directed toward promotions. For this you'll want to make a witch's ladder (a string of nine knots). While this particular component was used for various things, I like the symbolism here for "climbing the corporate ladder." As you bind each knot into the string (whose color you might want to choose for success, like red), speak your desire for an improved status at work into the knot. Then over the next nine weeks at work, untie one knot to slowly release the magical energy. When you're done, you can either reuse the string for similar magic or burn it with thankfulness for any improvements you've seen.

The third type of job magic seeks to stop the political mill that fills so many workplaces by binding gossip. To begin, write the name of the perpetrator on a bay leaf. Tie this into a white cloth, saying:

> With each knot that's tied, your lies I bind.
> Let truth come forth when you speak your mind!

Keep this in a safe place, where it won't be disturbed, in the office. If the leaf ever crumbles you'll need to replace it.

Throughout this chapter you've probably noticed that a lot of the incantations rhyme. This isn't necessary with your own adaptations, I just use it to make them easy to remember. After all, we can't be making charms and amulets all day long . . . we still have potions to brew!

⋛ six ⋐

Bubble, Bubble, Toil and Trouble
(Food and Beverage Magic)

She tasted of life's bitter cup;
refused to drink the potion up.

—old epitaph

This wicked witch *loves* to whip up a little magic in her kitchen, pantry and at the grill. So much of witchcraft's past centered around the hearth fire and household spices that it seems fitting to find me here, especially when my cat familiar (named Shaman) is twirling himself around my feet. One instance in particular comes to mind as I write. Picture this: a witch making ritual soap (something that bubbles a lot) in an iron pot that looks much like a cauldron. I'd become my own stereotype (all that was missing was the pointy black hat)!

Personal pleasures aside, kitchen magic is a great way for the time-challenged wicked witch to complete two tasks at once. Specifically, you can make a meal or beverage and stir up some productive power in the process! Since cooking is a kind of ritual unto itself, and many edibles in history had metaphysical correspondences, we can turn any breakfast, lunch, dinner or snack into a sumptuous, magical feast that soothes the heart, feeds the stomach, pleases the eye, tickles the fancy and strengthens the spirit!

The Crafty Kitchen

Before you can effectively use your wicked witchery to prepare magically enhanced foods and beverages, you first have to think of your kitchen in a little different light. During your witchy moments this space becomes a temple of sorts, where the sacred fires ignite at the stove! So, look around your kitchen right now. Does it have the ambience of a temple? Probably not, but that's because many witches have never approached it in that way before. All is not lost!

The main thing that sets apart a sacred space from an everyday countertop is your attitude. So, the first step in creating the wicked witch's kitchen is to move into your work area thoughtfully and purposefully. Light a candle, burn incense, chant, sing or do whatever makes the process feel more magical for you. I'd also suggest doing a little cleanup and organizational work too so you're not distracted by mundane clutter.

Next, choose your ingredients according to your goal(s) and good taste. (This kind of magic will do little if you can't stand the flavor of what you've created!) If you're working with a specific recipe, learn about the metaphysical energies of each ingredient so you can willfully (focus on your intent) mix them together, or substitute in a tasty, meaningful ingredient. For example, if a recipe called for soy sauce, but you wanted to use salt for protection and cleansing instead, you could decrease the amount of soy, and add a pinch of salt (soy is often used as a salt substitute).

Stir your mixture clockwise to draw positive energy. Stir counterclockwise to banish unwanted energy. Whip it to increase power, heat it up to create warm feelings, barbecue it as part of a fire festival or to burn away what it represents, microwave it to hasten manifestation, freeze it to cool anger or can it to preserve your magic. Really, the possibilities here are as endless as your imagination and culinary skills will allow.

By the way, witches need not be great chefs to work kitchen magic (thank goodness). Remember the KISS motto? Well, it applies to your pantry witchery too. You can fill boxed and canned food with witchy intentions just as surely as you can empower a lavish three-course meal. Think of it this way: When you open the can or box, you open the potential energy of the food. When you prepare it, you activate its potential! It's really that simple. Finally, eating or drinking internalizes the energy so it can fill your body, mind, aura and spirit. Talk about soul food!

Beverages

Despite what you've heard not all of the wicked witch's potions were unsavory or smelly. In fact, since people often drank these substances, the recipes we find in more reputable books sound downright tasty! About the only exception to this rule seems to be healing elixirs, which for some reason work best when they smell or taste terrible. If you don't believe me, just ask my friends who've tried my cold and flu tea. The aroma is akin to dirty sweatsocks, but the stuff works like a charm.

Some of the traditional witch's potions were based in water, while others were made from wine, beer, milk, juice and mead. Generally, alcoholic beverages were better than much of the drinking water of the time, and in health elixirs it covered up the taste and smell of the herbs.

Not all of the wicked witch's potions are consumed, however. Some might be poured out in libation as part of a ritual or spell, or to douse the sacred fires. Others might be used to asperge the sacred space, or as magically enhanced soil fertilizer (especially for the witch's garden). Still others can be boiled away to either disperse the energy they represent with the steam, or to destroy what they represent (like a liquid poppet, just take care not to burn the pot).

With this in mind, I strongly suggest you clearly label

every potion you make with the ingredients and instructions as to whether or not it's safe for consumption. Modern witches heed the rule of safety first. If one of the bottles breaks and a child or pet gets into the brew, you're going to want to know whether or not to take action. Additionally, if you work with a group, some of your witchy cohorts might be allergic to one or two ingredients. A simple label could save a life, or minimally make everyone more comfortable with the energies represented by the elixir.

Ingredient Correspondences for Wicked Potions

If you're not brewing for consumption, the ingredients for your potions are unlimited as long as they correspond to your magical goal (Rule One: Meaning is everything!). I do, however, recommend choosing ingredients that won't harm the earth or animals who might accidentally stumble across your libations. The calling of a wicked witch is one that always remains aware of our stewardship of this planet—even when it's not convenient, and perhaps even more so when it's not.

That said, I can only include a few recipes in a format like this for you to try. So, this potential component list (and the one for food items later in this chapter) will give you some ideas with which to begin. I've included several fruits and vegetables here (which can be juiced), spices with which to flavor them and other liquid bases, teas (herbs) and other ingredients that fare well when made into drinkable potions.

Potion Components and Magical Correspondences

Ale: Sacred to Isis and Hathor, use this to represent the fire element, for purifying potions. A dream of drinking beer portends a long life!

Allspice: Another fire element, sprinkle this spice into potions for prosperity and luck.

Apple: Sacred to Venus, Apollo and Zeus, use it to represent the water element. Add apple slices, apple juice or apple flavoring to elixirs for health, insight and love.

Banana: This fruit represents the air element and the masculine force of the universe (yang). Use in tonics for devotion, safety and to connect with the god aspect.

Blueberry: The water element. Add blueberries or their juice to items for peace and protection from evil energies.

Brandy: The fire element. Use brandy to appease spirits (perhaps dab it on yourself during divination or before a seance).

Carrot: The fire element and another masculine symbol. Add carrot juice to potions for passion, vision and grounding.

Celery: The fire element. Add celery to love libations and beverages aimed at improving the conscious mind.

Cinnamon: Sacred to Venus and Aphrodite because it's considered an aphrodisiac and is aligned with the fire element. Add to refreshments for energy, power, victory and lust.

Crystals: The earth element. While you obviously don't drink these, you can steep a clean crystal in water or other liquid base to create crystal elixirs that bear the vibrations of the chosen stone. The uses for these are determined by the crystal. For example, amethyst inspires self-discipline (which is why some people used to drink wine from an amethyst-carved cup).

Daisy: The water element. Add daisy petals to your spring wines to encourage youthful energy and prophetic ability.

Dandelion: The air element. Add dandelion leaves or flowers to beverages to help with wish manifestation and augment your awareness of spiritual entities.

Ginger: The fire element. Ginger provides a boost of successful energy to beverages, especially those for money and romance.

Grape: Sacred to Bacchus and Hathor, it represents the water element. Add to potions for celebratory rituals and to enhance abundant energies.

Honey: Sacred to Min and Artemis (among others), honey represents the air element. Use it to encourage joy, health, purity and spiritual awareness.

Lemon: The water element. Suited to potions prepared for friendship, fresh perspectives and longevity.

Milk: Sacred to Isis, Min and Zeus, it represents the element of water. Use milk as a base for potions aimed at connecting with the goddess or lunar energies.

Mint: The air element. Add to teas and tinctures to revitalize your energy, passion, sense of adventure, improve cash flow and generally provide zest.

Moon: The moon is a component to brewing magic for timing purposes. Make your potions by the full moon of October for the best energies (especially homemade wines and beers). Other potions might be created during a waning moon to banish, or a waxing moon to draw positive energy into the blend.

Nutmeg: Sacred to many god/desses in India, this spice represents the fire element. It's a good herb for fortune and fidelity brews.

Orange: The fire element. Add orange rind or juice to mixtures for love, good fortune, health and/or prosperity. Superstition says that chewing on orange rind before you imbibe offsets drunkenness by giving the drinker a boost of self-control.

Peach: The water element. Add peaches to freezes for wisdom, friendship and peace.

Pear: Sacred to Athena. Another water element, pear juice added to your beverages inspires zeal (especially with regard to relationships).

Pineapple: The fire element. Add pineapples as garnishes or pineapple juice to potions designed to incur hospitality, improve fidelity, protect or cleanse.

Raspberry: Sacred to Venus, the water element. Add this to protective beverages or those intended to inspire love.

Rose: Sacred to Venus, the water element. Add rose water or petals to elixirs for romance, love, divinatory ability and overall well-being.

Sage: Sacred to Zeus. Sage represents the air element and is excellent in magical beverages for improved wisdom, health, fitness, longevity and fertility.

Strawberry: Sacred to Freya, and a welcome fruit in my home any time, the strawberry represents the water element. Strawberries have lighthearted, profuse energy perfectly suited to the humor of wicked witchery.

Tea (black): The fire element, use tea as a basis for any potion to which you'd like to bring the energy of wealth, courage, strength, restfulness and physical vitality. Two notes of caution: Old, wise people tell us to put the tea into a beverage before any other ingredient to attract good luck, and that two women should never pour from the same pot unless one wants to conceive.

Vanilla: The water element. Use a vanilla bean to stir awareness, love or productivity potions.

Water: Folklore tells us that evil spirits are driven off by blessed water, so by all means bless your water-based potions (which also then become perfect for asperging the ritual space).

Whiskey: The fire element. According to American folklore, whiskey will remove curses, attract good energies and turn away ill-motivated spirits. You can steep herbs in whiskey for various effects.

Wine: Sacred to Ishtar, Osiris and Bacchus, this represents the fire element. Use it as a base for magical brews to which you want to bring a ritualistic feel, or for celebratory occasions. If you happen to spill a bit of this on yourself during the preparation process, it means improved fortune is on its way. Always pass your wines around the table clockwise to inspire blessings!

Note: For those of you who wish to avoid alcohol, the nonalcoholic versions of beer and wine may certainly be substituted. Do, however, consider if the elemental correspondence has changed from fire to water since the "fire" (alcohol) has been eliminated from the beverage.

Recipes

∋ Broken Heart Brew ∈

Make and drink this beverage to ease the pain of a broken heart. To improve the overall effect, mix the ingredients during a waning moon so that your sadness disappears by the next moon phase.

The berries in this recipe encourage happiness, brandy cleanses and rose inspires improved self-image and self-love.

1 cup elderberry wine
1 cup blackberry wine
1 cup brown sugar (or honey)

1 orange, sliced
1 cup fresh raspberries
1 apple, sliced
pinch of ginger
1–2 whole cloves
2 teaspoons rose water
1 cup brandy

Warm the wines with the brown sugar, orange, raspberries, apple, ginger and cloves, simmering them for 15 to 20 minutes. Do not boil. Remove the orange and apple, then allow the remainder to cool before pouring it into a glass bottle. Add the rose water and brandy. Shake this daily throughout the waning to dark moon phase, saying: "*As above, so below, let my heart become whole. As the moon disappears so will sadness and fear.*" Drink a cup of the beverage when the moon is dark to begin the healing process.

For those who prefer a nonalcoholic version of this, replace the wine with any personally enjoyed fruit juice, delete the brandy (you can substitute flavoring instead) and decrease the sweetening to personal taste.

⇥ Loving Honey Mead ⇤

This beverage accents peaceful, loving intentions. Drink it yourself (or with your beloved) just prior to meetings focused on romance, commitment and passion. Note that this is a beverage that needs to age after it's made.

In the interim, you can buy mead at a wine shop and add the appropriate herbs to it before serving.

By the way, the reason we call the period after a marriage a "honeymoon" is because it was often an entire month of celebration (one moon) in which the couple drank mead for longevity, fertility and passion.

    1 gallon apple juice
    8 whole cloves
    1 orange, sliced
    3 cinnamon sticks
    1 cup strawberries
    1 cup raspberries
    2 ½ pounds honey
    1 package champagne yeast
    2 tablespoons rose water
    ½ cup blanched almonds
    ½ vanilla bean, ground
    ¼-inch ginger root, pounded

Warm the apple juice in a nonaluminum pot over a low flame with the cloves, orange, cinnamon and berries. Once this is warm, add the honey and stir regularly until it's fully incorporated. Turn up the heat and boil the mixture for 5 minutes, skimming off the scum that rises to the top. Turn off the pot and strain the mixture.

Suspend the champagne yeast in ¼ cup of warm water for 15 minutes while the heated mixture cools. When the mead has reached room temperature, add the yeast and rose water, stirring once, and cover the pot with a heavy towel. Leave it for 3 days. Meanwhile, find a large glass bottle into which you can transfer the mead. Sterilize the bottle by boiling it for ten minutes. Put your almonds, vanilla bean and ginger in the bottom of this bottle. Pour the mead into the jar carefully, leaving behind any sediment that's already settled to the bottom of the pot (I find it helps to pour through cheesecloth).

Cover the top of the jar with a large balloon stretched across the opening (uninflated). This will keep the jar from exploding as fermentation occurs. Replace the balloon as necessary for the next 4 months. At this point you can strain the blend, and put a tight cap on the top. Store in a dark, cool area for another 3 to 4 months, then enjoy! Note: The longer you age your mead, the clearer and more potent it becomes, but it will also lose sweetness. So, if you prefer a dryer wine, let it age longer.

Those readers who choose not to imbibe can get nonalcoholic mead or simply make the above recipe decreasing the amount of honey to personal taste and eliminating the yeast. The resulting beverage can be served warm or cold immediately. The ingredients are essentially the same, so it won't lose magical meaningfulness.

⇥ Jealousy Juice ⇤

Jealousy can be very harmful to friendships and intimate relationships. If you find yourself being bitten by the green-eyed monster, and your worries are really unfounded, try drinking this juice on a Sunday, the day that supports magic for reasoning and logical perspectives.

The strawberries here stress love, cranberries protect you from your emotions, orange is for pure intention and mint and violet help still the jealousy bug who's biting at your heels.

>   1 cup strawberry juice (or juice blend)
>   ¼ cup cranberry juice
>   ¼ cup orange juice
>   2 fresh mint leaves (garnish)
>   1 fresh organically grown violet blossom
>   (garnish)

Mix the juices together and drink the entire batch. Nibble on the mint leaves and violet leaves afterward to keep your words gentle and kind, and to refresh your perspectives.

∋ Courage Coffee ∈

Need to grow a backbone and have some firm energy to support that mettle? This beverage should help, especially if allowed to steep in sunlight for a while to saturate it with power. If you prefer, you can use decaf in this recipe. Tea drinkers can substitute black tea for the flavored coffee.

>   1 pot banana-flavored coffee
>   (check the gourmet coffee section)
>   1 tumbled amber or carnelian stone
>   (clean)

Brew up your coffee at noon, which is when the sun is in its glory. If possible, put the coffeepot in the sunlight while the coffee is brewing. Solar energy augments magical efforts for strength, assurance and bravery. Place the amber or carnelian in the bottom of the coffeepot so the entire mixture gets the benefit of the stone's energies (just be careful not to pour it into your cup).

If you want this brew to last a little longer, you can add a little banana liqueur to the mix and drink it over several days. You can add a little cream to this in order to balance fortitude with sensitivity, or chill the blend to calm an overextended sense of confidence.

⇥ Retaliation Tea ⇤

Gearing up for magical retaliation? Want a clear mind and spirit with which to work? The herbs in this tea are designed to help you think and act with a distinct focus, leading to peace of mind and a sense of safety.

1 teaspoon anise seed
1 teaspoon black tea
1 cinnamon stick
1 teaspoon dried,
    organically grown violet leaves
¼ teaspoon rosemary
2 spearmint leaves
1 cup boiling water
1 cup crushed ice

Steep all the ingredients except the ice in the boiling water until it has a strong aroma (about 10 minutes). Strain into the cup of crushed ice (the ice here gives you a cool head with which to work). Stir the mixture clockwise saying, "*Within this potion my magic bind, grant to me an astute mind. Direct my focus and energies, by my will this spell is freed!*" Drink the potion up and get to work!

꒐ Trouble Tincture ꒐

You won't be drinking this beverage, but you'll want to store it in a dark, airtight container once it's made. That way you can pour away your troubles whenever they strike (refilling the bottle with a fresh batch of tincture as needed). Alternatively, sprinkle this around your sacred space to keep troublemakers away!

1 teaspoon mint
½ teaspoon basil
½ teaspoon rosemary
Handful fresh rose petals
1 slice orange
1 tablespoon sage
½ teaspoon angelica
½ teaspoon ginger root
1 slice lime
Pinch of salt
1 slice lemon
3 cups boiling water

¼ cup whiskey or rum
Agate, quartz or obsidian piece

Steep all these protective ingredients in the boiling water, then let it cool. Strain into your chosen container, adding the whiskey or rum (which helps preserve the tincture and also has a protective nature). Put your chosen crystal(s) in the bottom of the bottle, then cap it tightly. Use as needed, moving counterclockwise as you apply the liquid for banishing purposes. Perhaps add an incantation like, "*Bubble, bubble . . . no toils or troubles. All problems away, forever to stay!*"

⫤ Grief and Guilt Gargle ⫣

Another potion that you won't be drinking, but simply gargling with and spitting neatly down the drain. Grief and guilt often manifest in our words, so this action helps you literally spit out the negative feelings and send them away from you.

1 sprig sage
½ teaspoon rosemary
1 bay leaf
½ teaspoon thyme
1 teaspoon mint
1 cup hot water
2 tablespoons rum (optional)

Place the herbs in a tea ball or piece of cheese-cloth and steep them until the water takes on a tealike consistency (about 10 minutes). Take a small sip when it's lukewarm. Add sugar and rum to the blend if you find the flavor disagreeable (the sugar should sweeten your speech too!). Then gargle, keeping your purpose in mind as you purge the guilt or grief.

Foods

You know, I must confess that I never really thought about macaroni and cheese as having any magic to it. For that matter, I never considered roast beef, mashed potatoes and corn a great witchy treat . . . at least not until I became a wicked kitchen witch! Part of the inspiration for that change in my life came from reading *The Magic in Food* (Scott Cunningham), and writing *The Kitchen Witch's Cookbook*. Suddenly I couldn't go into my pantry and *not* see magical potential just waiting for me there. From that moment forward, my kitchen became a place where I feed my family's spirits with everything from soup to nuts, as well as their seemingly endless appetites! The information provided here should help you do likewise, with proper twists and temperaments suited to the wicked witch.

Ingredient Correspondences for Wicked Foods

As with beverages, you can bake magical items that are not for consumption by humans (like gifts for the bird spirits, magical edibles for your pets or offerings for the god/dess). But, I think most witches will use food magic to take in the energies they most need to internalize or radiate. If you think of the way digestion works—breaking down food and transporting its vitamins to every cell in your body—the symbolism here for magic is pretty powerful. Better still, symbolism can be tasty!

Here's a list of some common food items and their symbolic value for your magical menus. If a fruit or vegetable was included in the beverage list, I didn't repeat it here. This is obviously an abbreviated overview to which you should add healthy doses of personal insight and cultural flavor for best results.

Food Components and Magical Correspondences

Alfalfa sprouts: Alfalfa represents either the earth or water element, depending on the magical book you read. Add it to foods for providence, spiritual focus and improving prosperity.

Almonds: Sacred to Artemis and Mercury. The air element. Sprinkle into prosperity, love and wisdom recipes.

Bamboo shoots: The air and water elements. Stir-fry up some longevity and safety.

Barley: Sacred to Indra and Demeter. The earth element. Blend into relationships stews and pain reduction (emotional, mental or physical) soups.

Basil: Sacred to Vishnu. The fire element. Use this spice for banishing, protection, love and prosperity.

Bay: Sacred to Apollo and Ceres. The fire element. Add a bay leaf to improve insight (especially spiritual) or augment physical strength and vitality.

Beans: Sacred to Demeter. The air element. Eat beans before fortune-telling efforts (especially to improve your ability to communicate what you see in a reading). Also a symbol of abundance.

Beef: Sacred to Hathor. The earth element. Beef supports energy for wealth, building foundations or grounding out excess energy.

Beets: Sacred to Aphrodite. The earth element. Beet juice is a suitable blood substitute for older spells, and represents love, passion or attractiveness.

Bread: Sacred to Isis. The earth element. As the staff of life, bread symbolizes providence, friendship, family, unity and life's continuance.

Broccoli: Sacred to Jupiter. The water element. A good vitality food. Also supports authority, health and safety.

Butter: The earth element (some water). Spread this on liberally when making peace with people, attempting to persevere through a situation or resolving issues.

Cheese: Sacred to Apollo. The earth element (some water). Since Roman times, cheese has been used for nurturing relationships, happiness and well-being. It's also a manifestation munchie.

Chicken: The earth or fire element. Make old-fashioned chicken soup when you want improved health or as part of solar celebrations.

Coconut: Sacred to Athena and Ganymede. The water element. Coconut is well suited to energizing foods with magic, psychic sensitivity and adaptability.

Corn: Sacred to Cerridwen. The earth/fire element. Corn represents prosperity, providence, harvest magic and Spirit's presence.

Crab: Sacred to Apollo. The water/earth element. Crabmeat protects the consumer from evil and disease; it's also an aphrodisiac (note: consider cleaning and retaining the shell as a charm).

Dill: Sacred to Shiva. The element of fire. Dill promotes safety (especially for children), prosperity and passion.

Egg: Sacred to Venus. The central element of Spirit. Eggs encourage manifestation, beginnings, hope, fertility and rebirth.

Fish: Sacred to Neptune. The water element. Fish is a well-known fertility food that is said to also aid with sexual prowess and help bring about abundance.

Fruit: Sacred to Gaia. The elemental correspondences vary, as do associations, but fruit furthers happiness, fertility and prosperity.

Garlic: Sacred to Hecate. The fire element. Eat garlic (followed by breath mints) for protection, banishing unwanted energy, to turn magic and for spirit warding.

Lettuce: The water element. Lettuce is considered a lunar food that attracts money and tranquility.

Marjoram: Sacred to Venus. The air element. Marjoram protects the consumer from evil, improves your love life and sustains health.

Olive: Sacred to Minerva, Apollo and Ra. The air element. Olive fosters positive communications in sexuality and other pleasures. It also advances harmony and peace.

Pepper: The fire element. Pepper is considered nearly universally as a cleansing, protecting herb because of its biting nature.

Pork: Sacred to Carnea. The earth element. Pork grounds excess energy, is suited to spring rituals and promotes fecundity.

Rice: The air element. In the Far East particularly, rice is consumed for luck, abundance, long life and banishing ill-motivated spirits/people.

Salt: Sacred to Osiris and Neptune. The earth element. Use salt to purify, protect, cleanse or to encourage honesty and trust. In Arabic tradition, it represents hospitality and consideration.

Soup: Sacred to Cerridwen. The central Spirit element. Soup blends diverse energies into a harmonious whole. It's also very suited to inspiring creativity and inventiveness.

Walnut: The fire element. Add walnuts to recipes that are aimed at manifesting wishes, emphasizing the conscious mind or increasing physical fertility.

Yogurt: The water element. Yogurt augments spiritual pursuits, the nurturing instinct and the goddess.

Recipes

⊰ Apathy Apples ⊱

One of the things that often hinders magic and truly fulfilling wicked witchery is being stung by the apathy bug. Next time that happens, make this dish and sting back with bountiful energy and a healthier outlook! This dish is also nice as part of autumn postritual feasts, having all the right ingredients for nurturing enthusiasm. (Serves 6 adults.)

> 3 cups of peeled apples, thinly sliced
> 1 tablespoon flour and ¼ teaspoon ginger
>   powder, blended
> 1 standard one-crust pie crust
> ½ teaspoon finely grated orange rind
> ½ teaspoon finely grated lemon zest
>   (optional)
> ½ cup slivered almonds
> 1 cup brown sugar
> ¼ stick butter

Toss the apple slices with the flour and ginger blend until they're evenly coated. Lay these out evenly on one half of the pie crust. Next, mix the orange rind, lemon zest, almonds and brown sugar and sprinkle this over the top of the apples. Dab with butter evenly. Fold the pie crust over the apple mix and secure the edges by pinching (this configuration creates a womb in which your magic grows toward manifestation).

Make a few fork holes in the top of the tart, then bake in a preheated 350-degree oven for 40 minutes, or until the crust is golden brown and juice bubbles up through the fork holes. Serve with a sprinkling of sweet cream (to nurture yourself).

⊰ Depression Dandelion and Petal-power Salad ⊱

Even the best wicked witch has "down" days. This whimsical, vitamin-packed salad should lift your spirits. Also consider serving this during late spring festivals.

For vegetarians in particular, edible flowers represent a marvelous way to infuse your diet with beauty and magical power! Make sure they've been grown without pesticides. (Serves 6 adults.)

    4 good-size handfuls of dandelion greens,
        washed (for perspective)
    A sprinkling of daisy petals, washed
        (for a return to innocence and hope)
    1 handful of rose petals, washed (for self-love)
    1 handful of carnation petals, washed
        (for pride and confidence)
    ¼ cup wine vinegar
    ½ cup olive oil
    ½ teaspoon of any of *one* of the following:
        garlic, ginger, onion, rosemary, thyme,
        crushed raspberries
    Pinch of salt and sugar

Gently toss the first four ingredients in a bowl. In a separate container, blend the remaining ingredients for the vinaigrette. As you pour and mix this into the petals, visualize them being filled with a refreshing yellow, white and pale blue light for creativity and happiness. Nibble expectantly!

⋑ Love Linguini ⋐

Feeling a little insecure with your mate, or just want to put a little zest back into a relationship? Make you and your significant other this wonderful pasta dish. As you eat it, internalize self-love, then turn those warm energies toward each other! Just remember to serve breath mints after the meal! (Serves 2 adults.)

> 1 6-ounce can minced clams
> ¾ cup diced crabmeat
> 2 cloves freshly chopped garlic
> 1 teaspoon oregano
> 2 tablespoons butter
> 2 tablespoons white cooking wine
> 1 cup diced canned tomatoes
> 2 servings cooked linguini
> Freshly grated Asiago or Parmesan cheese
> Salt and pepper to taste

Place the clams, crabmeat, garlic, oregano and butter together in a small pan and sauté them over a low flame until the room is filled with aromatic anticipation and the garlic is golden. Add the cooking wine and tomatoes. Toss gently as you think warm, romantic thoughts. Pour this over the linguini, sprinkling the cheese and salt and pepper on top; serve in a candlelit room with a heaping side order of amorous music.

Note that if you have intense passion in mind, you might want to substitute oysters for the crab, and some chopped celery and onion to the sauté mixture; garnish with parsley.

⩰ Sour Disposition Sweets ⩰

I must confess that I'm a junk-food junkie. I love sweet treats, but this one begins with something very healthy for you: citrus rinds. Since these tend to be tart, the candying process accomplishes symbolically what you hope to do internally—sweeten things up! Try to use organically grown citrus, as the rind is where the pesticides reside. (Makes 6 to 8 large candies that can be cut up into 24 to 30 smaller pieces.)

Rind from 2 lemons
Rind from 2 limes
Rind from 2 oranges
Rind from 1 pink grapefruit
5 cups boiling water
2 cups honey
1 teaspoon rose water
1 teaspoon vanilla
1 teaspoon ginger
Sugar

Take the citrus rinds you've collected and remove as much of the white inner skin as you can. This is very important, so take your time. Don't forget to focus on your goal while you're working.

Next, cut the rinds so that they're in half-inch strips. While you're doing this, fill a large, nonaluminum pan with the water and bring it to a boil. Put your cut rinds into the boiling water for 10 minutes. Drain them and then boil with fresh water for another ten minutes (this lessens the tartness and makes them more tender).

In another pan mix the honey, rose water, vanilla and ginger with ½ cup of water. Warm this mixture until the honey is liquefied and the spices are well blended. Put your boiled fruit rinds into the honey mixture, keeping it over a low flame. Cook these for about an hour, watching closely to avoid any burning.

Remove the rinds from the honey and spread them on wax paper to dry, with another piece of wax paper placed loosely on top. Turn these regularly while they dry, scattering a little white sugar over each one on each side as you turn them. These morsels last nearly indefinitely. Just keep them in a canister and nibble a bite any time you need to improve your disposition.

Note: If you often need extra energy, this process works for thinly sliced ginger root too.

⇥ Ham It Up Ham ⇤

In Chapter 1, we talked about the fact that wicked witches aren't shy about bringing a dramatic flair to magic and daily life. From experience, however, I know it's sometimes hard to muster that thespian spirit. So, this recipe encourages us to "ham" it up using ham as a foundation. For vegetarians, I suggest substituting sweet potatoes (considering them as a poppet to represent the ham). (Serves 1.)

> 1 ham slice cooked to your liking
> 1 teaspoon maple syrup
>   (for life's sweetness)
> Pinch rosemary
>   (for playful, youthful outlooks)
> Pineapple chunks
>   (to be well received)

Place the ham slice in an oven-safe pan and top it with the syrup, rosemary and pineapple. Place it in the oven, saying: "*All the world is a stage, and I have a part to play. Give me the power of flamboyance today!*" Warm the ham at 300 degrees until it sizzles with your magic (about 20 minutes), then enjoy.

⇥ Passionate Strawberry Chicken ⇤

This is my favorite recipe of all time for summer fire festivals that begin and end at the grill. The berries and honey in the mix create all the right energies for romance and passion to blossom after the meal is over. Vegetarians may substitute large mushroom caps for the chicken in this recipe. (Serves 4 to 6 adults.)

12 ounces frozen strawberries with juice
(unsweetened)
¼ cup wine vinegar
1 teaspoon garlic powder
1 teaspoon ginger powder
1 teaspoon onion powder
2 tablespoons Worcestershire sauce
2 tablespoons soy sauce
6 skinless, boneless chicken breasts
1 tablespoon chopped garlic
(or to taste)
1 cup honey

Defrost the strawberries. Pour the juice into a large food-storage container with a secure lid, and set the berries aside for later. To the juice add the vinegar, garlic powder, ginger powder, onion powder, Worcestershire and soy. Note that you can adjust these ingredients to suit personal taste. Stir well.

Take the chicken breasts and rinse them. Make small holes in the surface of the meat with a fork, rinsing in cold water again. Put them into the juice and spice mixture. Put the container's top on, and return everything to the refrigerator for at least 4 hours. Turn the meat or shake the container regularly.

Drain off the marinade and add the chopped garlic, half the drained strawberries and the honey to it. Fire up your barbecue grill (put it on a low setting).

Put the meat on the grill, heating each side once (about 7 minutes each, depending on your grill and the size of the chicken breasts) before applying the honey mixture.

Liberally coat each side with the honey and spices each time you turn the meat until it's cooked all the way through. (Note: Always turn the meat toward the right to attract positive energy to the process.) Serve with a garnish of strawberries or berries and cream for dessert. Eat creatively!

⊰ Vital Vegetables ⊱

Many vegetables are considered healthful medically and metaphysically. This spicy vegetable blend adds a little herb power to the equation for well-being and vitality. After all, a healthy witch is a happy witch! (Serves 4 adults.)

¼ cup olive oil
1 tablespoon chopped garlic
¼ cup diced red onion
1 head chopped broccoli, presteamed
   (slightly crunchy)
4 carrots, chopped and presteamed
   (still slightly crunchy)
½ teaspoon grated orange
   (fruit and rind; use organically
   grown oranges)
1 cup pine nuts or walnuts
   (your choice)

Warm the olive oil in a wok or similar type frying pan. Add the garlic and onion, sautéing until both are lightly browned. If you wish, add an incantation at this time like, "Vitality, grow in me!" Toss the broccoli and carrots into the herb blend, heating for 2 to 3 minutes, turning regularly. Stir in the orange and nuts and serve as is or over a bed of rice.

As you can see, it's not overly difficult to get wicked in the kitchen with just a little creativity. Really, there's nothing unique about these beverages and foods other than the thoughtfulness and intentions you put into them!

Afterword

An unwritten rule of wicked witchery is to always get in the last word! Since I try to follow the guidelines I give others, these are my final words on the subject of being a wicked witch. A lot of people ask me why I would write a book that seems, on the surface, to focus on a negative portrait (i.e., the traditional wicked witch). My answer to that is simple: to reclaim a negative and make it into something positive for both our mundane and our spiritual lives.

Witchcraft has undergone many changes in recent years, not the least of which is opening its broom closet to the public eye. In the process, more of us have been able to share our faith with greater freedom. Yet, we still face a lot of old stereotypes and opposition. We can either embrace those obstacles and use them for our betterment or keep punching the proverbial brick wall. I choose the former solution.

Since I suspect witches still have some years ahead of them where they will face misunderstandings, our magic's power to "turn and change" is nothing less than essential. So, modern witchery is focused on transformation—turning any situation into something that is life-affirming, empowering, fulfilling and fun. If you read the last sentence and asked, "How?" go back and read Chapter 1 again. You missed something important.

Being a wicked witch is also about wearing the "witch" title proudly, even if that only means the sly, knowing smile displayed on our faces. Modern witches recognize that changing people's feelings about magic won't happen overnight. It's not our place to shove witchery down people's throats, or even convince other witches of the validity of our way of practicing. Nonetheless, with time and tenacity, there will come a day when the word "witch" will inspire hope and respect from outsiders, and within our circles we'll rediscover peace.

Along the same lines, the wicked witch's philosophy encourages us to know ourselves, live proactively, reach out to others, honor the earth and look skyward toward the possibilities that stretch the boundaries of our imagination and our magick. In effect, the modern witchcraft movement encourages us to grasp our lives' control systems and get, well, witchy! It is, quite simply, living the magic every moment of every day.

Blessings to you wherever witchery takes you, by foot, by car or by broom.

About the Author

Trish Telesco is a folk magician of fifteen-plus years and the author of fifty Wiccan and neo-Pagan books. She currently lives in western New York with her family and pets, enjoying landscaping, cooking, antique restoration and various craft projects in her spare time. Trish considers herself a keep-it-simple witch who values vision and creativity as essential to spiritual growth. Her current projects include designing spiritually oriented tours of Europe (see www.lorsinger.com) and supporting important neo-Pagan causes, including a land fund (www.phoenixfestivals.com) and a building fund (www.dragonhills.com). She travels a minimum of twice a month, giving lectures and workshops around the country, and can also be found regularly on the Internet at sites like www.clubs.yahoo.com/clubs/folkmagicwithtrish telesco and on www.witchvox.com.

Printed in the United States
By Bookmasters